IMAGES OF

UNITED STATES NAVY DESTROYERS

RARE PHOTOGRAPHS FROM WARTIME ARCHIVES

Michael Green

Pen & Sword

MARITIME

First published in Great Britain in 2020 by
PEN & SWORD MARITIME
An imprint of
Pen & Sword Books Ltd
47 Church Street
Barnsley
South Yorkshire
S70 2AS

ISBN 978-1-52675-854-5

Typeset by Concept, Huddersfield, West Yorkshire HD4 5JL.
Printed and bound in India by Replika Press Pvt. Ltd.

Pen & Sword Books Limited incorporates the imprints of Atlas, Archaeology, Aviation, Discovery, Family History, Fiction, History, Maritime, Military, Military Classics, Politics, Select, Transport, True Crime, Air World, Frontline Publishing, Leo Cooper, Remember When, Seaforth Publishing, The Praetorian Press, Wharncliffe Local History, Wharncliffe Transport, Wharncliffe True Crime and White Owl.

For a complete list of Pen & Sword titles please contact
PEN & SWORD BOOKS LIMITED
47 Church Street, Barnsley, South Yorkshire S70 2AS, England
E-mail: enquiries@pen-and-sword.co.uk
Website: www.pen-and-sword.co.uk

Contents

Dedication

The author dedicates this book to Medal of Honor winner Elmer Charles Bigelow of the US Navy. His citation reads as follows:

For conspicuous gallantry and intrepidity at the risk of his life above and beyond the call of duty while serving on board the USS *Fletcher* during action against enemy Japanese forces off Corregidor Island in the Philippines, February 14, 1945. Standing topside when an enemy shell struck the *Fletcher*, Bigelow, acting instantly as the deadly projectile exploded into fragments which penetrated the No. 1 gun magazine and set fire to several powder cases, picked up a pair of fire extinguishers and rushed below in a resolute attempt to quell the raging flames. Refusing to waste the precious time required to don rescue-breathing apparatus, he plunged through the blinding smoke billowing out of the magazine hatch and dropped into the blazing compartment. Despite the acrid, burning powder smoke which seared his lungs with every agonizing breath, he worked rapidly and with instinctive sureness and succeeded in quickly extinguishing the fires and in cooling the cases and bulkheads, thereby preventing further damage to the stricken ship. Although he succumbed to his injuries on the following day, BIGELOW, by his dauntless valor, unfaltering skill and prompt action in the critical emergency, had averted a magazine explosion which undoubtedly would have left his ship wallowing at the mercy of the furiously pounding Japanese guns on Corregidor, and his heroic spirit of self-sacrifice in the face of almost certain death enhanced and sustained the highest traditions of the United States Naval Service. He gallantly gave his life in the service of his country.

Introduction

In May 1898, the American Congress authorized the construction of sixteen destroyers. Before America's official entry into the First World War, the US Navy procured sixty-three destroyers divided into nine different classes. The last five classes were collectively referred to as 'broken-deckers' due to their high forecastle or 'thousand-tonners' due to their displacement.

Keenly aware of the threat posed by the German U-boats in the First World War, the American Congress authorized 267 destroyers. Only forty-one entered service before that conflict concluded. The remainder were completed by 1922. Due to the majority having four smoke stacks, they received the nickname 'four-stackers' or 'four-pipers'.

Beginning in 1932, up until the Japanese attack on Pearl Harbor, the US Navy placed into service ten new classes of destroyers totalling 169 units. During the war years, American shipyards built 334 destroyers, divided into three classes. The most numerous were the 175 examples of the *Fletcher* class: the most successful destroyer design of the Second World War.

During the Cold War, the threat from the Soviet Navy's submarine fleet pushed the development of seven new destroyer designs into service between 1949 and 1988, beginning with the *Mitscher* class and eventually into the stealth-shaped *Arleigh Burke* class of which eighty-two units are planned. The intended replacement for the *Arleigh Burke* class by 2020 was to be the first of thirty-two examples of the futuristic-looking *Zumwalt* class. However, cost overrides led to the class's cancellation in 2009 with only three to be built.

Acknowledgements

The historical images in this work come from the files of the US Navy Historical Center. The contemporary photographs come from a US Navy website. Some pictures came from friends that are named. As with all published works, authors depend on friends for assistance in reviewing their work.

Notes to the Reader

1. This book is not a comprehensive history of US Navy destroyers, but rather a broad overview of the subject.
2. All standard ship displacements are in long tons (2,240lb to the ton).
3. Stated displacements only represent a point in time of a destroyer's service with the US Navy due to ongoing alterations and upgrades.

Chapter One

Early Development

Atechnology breakthrough occurred in 1866 with British inventor Robert Whitehead's invention of the world's first self-propelled torpedo. A severe threat to battleships, then the dominant vessel in the world's navies and the symbol of maritime power, torpedoes were viewed as a real game-changer in naval warfare.

Navies around the world quickly began designing and building small, short-ranged, torpedo-armed surface vessels to challenge any hostile fleets approaching their shores. These new naval vessels unsurprisingly became known as 'torpedo boats'. Submarines, too, became torpedo-launching platforms.

US Navy Torpedo Boats

In 1886, the American Congress authorized construction of a 'first-class torpedo boat'. It entered service in 1890 as the USS *Cushing*, or Torpedo Boat No. 1 (TB-1). Its three onboard torpedoes had a maximum range of about 1,767 yards. *Cushing*'s only other armament consisted of three small-calibre deck guns.

The USS *Cushing* had a crew of twenty-two men and was 140ft long with a maximum beam of 15ft 1in. The vessel's displacement came in at 105 tons. Coal-fired boilers provided steam to two direct-drive, 'triple-expansion, reciprocating steam-powered engines'. The ship had a top speed of 23 knots, making it fast enough to chase down and engage slower warships such as battleships.

Of the thirty-five torpedo boats that the US Navy eventually took into service, twenty survived long enough to see service during the First World War (1914–18). All except one example were decommissioned and sold for scrap in 1919. The US

Displacement

The US Navy definition of displacement is the weight of the water displaced by a warship. Displacement is a constant for a given water density because the volume (subject to temperature and pressure) is a constant. The listed weights of each destroyer class described in this book fall under the heading of 'standard displacement'. It describes a fully-manned and armed warship, but does not include fuel and feedwater.

Navy decommissioned its last torpedo boat in 1925 and then sold it for scrap, the typical end for most warships.

Countering the Torpedo Boats

Reflecting a huge investment in fleets of battleships, the major navies of the world sought an effective countermeasure to the threat posed by torpedo boats, leading to the development of what initially became known as 'torpedo-boat destroyers'.

Torpedo-boat destroyers were to be larger and longer-ranged than torpedo boats, and better-armed. In theory, they could engage and destroy enemy torpedo boats before the latter could come sufficiently close to employ their weapons. Torpedo-boat destroyers' larger size allowed navies to mount torpedo tubes on them and, most importantly, accompany a fleet's capital ships at sea.

The keel of the first US Navy torpedo-boat destroyer, USS *Bainbridge*, was laid down in August 1899; she also became known as Torpedo Boat Destroyer No. 1 (TBD-1). Commissioned in November 1902, the ship had a crew of seventy-three and was 250ft long with a maximum beam of 23ft. Twelve additional *Bainbridge*-class torpedo-boat destroyers were commissioned into US Navy service by late 1903. The other three destroyers of the first sixteen acquired by the US Navy became the *Truxtun* class. Some reference sources divide the first thirteen destroyers of the *Bainbridge* class into different sub-classes.

USS *Bainbridge*'s displacement was 410 tons. Coal-fired boilers provided steam for her two direct-drive, triple-expansion, reciprocating steam-powered engines. The ship's maximum speed proved to be 29 knots. Smoke and gases from her four coal-fired boilers exited via four smokestacks ('stacks' in US Navy nomenclature).

Armament on the *Bainbridge* and *Truxtun* classes was generally similar, consisting of two torpedo tubes with two reload torpedoes stored onboard, and a few small-calibre deck guns including a 3in/23 gun. The first number represents the bore width and the second the calibre. Multiplying the gun's calibre by its bore width calculates the length of the weapon's barrel. Bore diameters for guns with a bore smaller than 3in are generally measured in millimetres.

Service Issues

Almost all of the US Navy's first sixteen torpedo-boat destroyers, authorized in 1898, had design problems that affected their operational performance. The primary reason was the inexperience of the majority of firms awarded the contracts to build them. A second issue proved to be the unrealistic maximum speed specifications required by the US Navy.

US Navy Commander C.M. Winslow reported his impressions on the US Navy's initial order of torpedo boats and torpedo-boat destroyers in an August 1904 report to President Theodore Roosevelt: 'The history of nearly all our torpedo boats and torpedo-boat destroyers has been that immediately after being delivered they have gone to the navy yard for repairs and alterations. They have rarely been run at any speed approximating the contract speed, and are almost continuously under repairs.'

Despite their design and reliability shortcomings, the US Navy's original sixteen torpedo-boat destroyers saw extensive service, including patrol stints in the Far East and around the Philippines. Two went to Panama as dispatch vessels. All would play some part in the First World War, but never engaged the enemy in combat.

In 1919, following the First World War, the US Navy decommissioned its first sixteen torpedo-boat destroyers and sold fourteen for scrap. The remaining two were sold and converted into commercial vessels.

New Label and Impressions

As time went on the label of torpedo-boat destroyer gave way to the more succinct name of 'destroyer'. In 1920, all US Navy destroyers were re-designated with the two-letter prefix 'DD', with TBD-1 relabelled 'DD-1' as an example. That same letter prefix and sequential number system would appear for subsequent destroyer classes.

US Navy Commander S.M. Robinson summed up his favourable impressions of the first sixteen destroyers taken into service in a 1920 US Navy report by stating: '[They] proved conclusively that the destroyer was a reliable seagoing vessel and had a cruising radius that compared favorably with other types of ship. The fuel economy at low speed was the greatest surprise of all.'

Order of 1906

It took until June 1906 before Congress authorized the next five destroyers for the US Navy to be eventually labelled as the *Smith* class (DD-17 through to DD-21). Commissioned between 1909 and 1919, they were the first US Navy destroyers powered by 'steam turbine engines' instead of triple-expansion, reciprocating steam-powered engines of previous destroyer classes.

The five new *Smith*-class destroyers each displaced 700 tons and was manned by a crew of eighty-seven men. Each had a length of 293ft 10in and a beam of 26ft. Top

---

Steam Turbine Engines

Steam turbine engines had many advantages over the older-generation, triple-expansion, reciprocating steam-powered engines. Steam turbine engines are capable of generating higher ship speeds due to their greater thermal efficiency, providing a higher power-to-weight ratio. Steam turbine engines could also keep up their maximum speed for much longer than triple-expansion, reciprocating steam engines, which was even more important than the top speed. Steam turbine engines also took up less space in warships and were more reliable.

speed came in at 28 knots. The steam turbine engines of the *Smith*-class destroyers continued to rely on coal-fired boilers, as had the first sixteen US Navy destroyers.

More Destroyers are Authorized

Congress authorized the first ten of what would become the twenty-one destroyers of the *Paulding* class (DD-22 through to DD-42) in 1908. Considered improved versions of the preceding five *Smith*-class destroyers, they generally shared the same overall design and operational characteristics.

The twenty-one *Paulding*-class destroyers had fuel oil-fired boilers instead of the coal-fired boilers used in all the previous destroyer classes. From an article titled 'Naval Innovation: From Coal to Oil' by Erik J. Dahl published in the winter 2000–2001 issue of *Joint Force Quarterly* appears this passage on the benefits of fuel oil for warships:

> Oil offered many benefits. It had double the thermal content of coal so that boilers could be smaller and ships could travel twice as far. Greater speed was possible and oil burned with less smoke so the fleet would not reveal its presence as quickly. Oil could be stored in tanks anywhere, allowing more efficient design of ships, and it could be transferred through pipes without reliance on stokers, reducing manning.

With the new powerplant arrangement, the *Paulding*-class engines produced more shaft horsepower (shp) than those on the previous *Smith*-class destroyers. Maximum speed on the *Paulding*-class destroyers rose to 29.5 knots.

Both the *Smith*- and *Paulding*-class destroyers fell under the unofficial general heading of 'flivvers' when the next more substantial and heavier class of US Navy destroyer began entering service in 1913. At the time, the term was American slang for a small, lightweight and cheap car that shook a lot, such as the famous Ford Model T. Some in the US Navy saw similarities between the two types of machines. All the flivvers were decommissioned in 1919 following the First World War, with a few sold for commercial use.

Larger Destroyers

Following the twenty-one *Paulding*-class destroyers there came out of the shipyards another twenty-six destroyers (DD-43 through to DD-68) divided among five classes. These comprised four of the *Cassin* class, four of the *Aylwin* class, six of the *O'Brien* class, six of the *Tucker* class and six of the *Sampson* class.

All destroyers of these five classes were generally similar in dimensions and personnel complements. With all having a displacement of just over 1,000 tons they were usually referred to by their unofficial nickname as the 'thousand-tonner' type or 'broken-deckers' due to their high forecastle.

The *Cassin* class came out of the shipyards between 1912 and 1915. Built at the same time as these vessels were the four near-identical destroyers of the *Aylwin* class (DD-47 through to DD-50). The latter went into production between 1912 and 1914. They had a top speed of 29.6 knots.

As the steam turbine engines in the US Navy's destroyers operated more efficiently at higher speed and less so at lower speeds, to maximize their range when operating at speeds of 15 knots and below, both the *Cassin* and *Aylwin* classes had back-up engines. In the case of the *Cassin* class they were triple-expansion, reciprocating engines, while the *Aylwin* class had compound, reciprocating steam-powered engines.

Powerplant Changes

The practice of fitting one or more back-up steam-powered engines into most of the thousand-tonner-type destroyers powered by direct-drive steam turbine engines continued through five of the six destroyers of the *O'Brien* class. The construction of the class (DD-51 through to DD-56) took place between 1913 and 1915.

The USS *Cushing* (DD-55), an *O'Brien*-class destroyer, differed from her five counterparts as she appeared with two new specially-designed 'cruising turbines' instead of the back-up engine/s installed on the other ships of her class. Top speed of the *O'Brien* class was 29 knots.

After the *O'Brien* class there appeared six destroyers of the *Tucker* class (DD-57 through to DD-62) built between 1914 and 1916. Like the USS *Cushing* (DD-55) of the previous *O'Brien* class, they had cruising turbines for more economical cruising speeds.

The only one of the five *Tucker*-class destroyers not having cruising turbines proved to be the USS *Wadsworth* (DD-60) which lacked any back-up engine or engines for more economical cruising speeds. Instead, ships' steam turbine engines were no longer directly coupled to the ship's propeller shafts as on previous destroyers. Instead, they coupled to reduction gears, which turned the ship's propeller shafts.

The last of the thousand-tonner types, the six destroyers of the *Sampson* class (DD-63 through to DD-68), retained direct-drive steam turbine engines with cruising

---

Reduction Gears

A reduction gear is a transmission employed to allow both steam turbine engines and ship propellers to operate within their most effective ranges of revolutions per minute (rpm). In other words, reduction gears reduce the high rpm of a steam turbine engine to the much lower RPMs of propeller shafts. The ratio of reduction is determined by the maximum efficiency obtainable from the propellers without loss of power at varying steam turbine engines and propeller speeds.

turbines, as did five of the *Tucker*-class destroyers. The *Sampson*-class destroyers came out of the shipyards between 1915 and 1917. Both the *Tucker*- and *Sampson*-class destroyers had a top speed of just under 30 knots.

Flivver Armament

The five destroyers of the *Smith* class (DD-17 through to DD-21) had five 3in guns and three single traversable torpedo-firing tubes. The latter each contained a single 18in-diameter torpedo. The ship had onboard stowage space for three reload torpedoes.

The twenty-one destroyers of the follow-on *Paulding* class (DD-22 through to DD-42), based on the previous *Smith* class, retained the same five 3in guns. On each destroyer three twin-mount torpedo-firing tubes replaced the three single-tube firing mounts and eliminated the reload torpedoes.

The majority of the flivver destroyers would eventually go to sea with depth-charges for service overseas during the First World War. This reflected the severe threat posed to allied merchant ships by the German Navy submarine fleet during the conflict.

Thousand-Ton-Type Armament

The first and second classes of the thousand-ton destroyer type, the *Cassin* and *Aylwin* (DD-43 through to DD-50) shared the same armament configuration. It consisted of four 4in/50 (102mm) deck guns and four twin-mount traversable torpedo-firing tubes.

As an experiment in 1917, one of the four *Aylwin*-class destroyers had its four single-mount 4in/50 deck guns replaced with four twin-mount 4in/50 deck guns. They quickly disappeared and the original single 4in/50 gun mounts went back on. As of 1929, all but one of the four *Aylwin*-class destroyers appeared with a single 3in anti-aircraft gun. The 4in/50 deck guns lacked the necessary elevation to perform as anti-aircraft guns.

Following the near-identical *Cassin* and *Aylwin* destroyers (DD-43 through to DD-50), the US Navy commissioned six destroyers of the *O'Brien* class (DD-51 through to DD-56). They were only slightly different from the two preceding classes. Their only significant improvement would be in their traversable torpedo tube-firing mounts now modified to permit the launching of 21in-diameter torpedoes rather than the previous 18in-diameter torpedoes.

The six *Tucker*-class destroyers' armament was identical to that of the *O'Brien* class. The last six destroyers of the thousand-ton type were the *Sampson* class. The four 4in/50 deck guns going back to the first destroyer of the thousand-ton types remained on the *Sampson* class. It would be their torpedo armament configuration that changed. The four sets of torpedo-firing tubes went from two tubes to three tubes each, bringing each ship's torpedo count to twelve.

Service Use

The US Navy's newest destroyers when the United States officially entered the First World War on 17 April 1917 were of the thousand-ton type. They would also be the first to enter the overseas war zone on 6 May 1917. Their assigned roles included anti-submarine patrols, convoy escort and rescue operations involving the crews of allied merchant ships sunk by German submarines. For the anti-submarine role, they appeared with depth-charges, as had the flivvers. There was no sonar available for the ships at that time.

Of the thousand-ton-type US Navy destroyers that served overseas during the First World War, none managed to account for a German submarine. However, on 6 December 1917, a German submarine sank the USS *Jacob Jones* (DD-61), a *Tucker*-class destroyer, the first US Navy destroyer sunk in combat. After the First World War the thousand-ton types went into reserve status.

A total of twelve of the thousand-ton type would go on to see a second career with the United States Coast Guard. Their job was to aid in enforcing 'Prohibition', the banning of all alcohol in the United States between 1920 and 1933. Known as the 'Rum Patrol', the former US Navy destroyers were tasked with intercepting liquor-smuggling mother ships at sea before they distributed their cargo to smaller faster boats that brought the alcohol ashore.

With the end of Prohibition in the United States, all the former destroyers went back to the US Navy between 1933 and 1934. With no further use for the thousand-ton types, the US Navy had all of them scrapped between 1934 and 1936 except for a single example. That ship was the USS *Allen* (DD-66), a *Sampson*-class destroyer that remained in service through to the end of the Second World War primarily in secondary roles, such as a training ship.

Caldwell-Class Destroyers

As already mentioned, the German submarine threat in the early years of the First World War was of intense concern to the allied war effort. The senior leadership of the US Navy had no doubts that America would soon enter into the conflict. This led to a demand in 1916 for a large number of destroyers for the anti-submarine (ASW) role.

Rather than have a new destroyer class designed especially for the ASW role, the Navy decided to save time by modifying the existing destroyer design for the *Caldwell* class. That class (DD-69 through to DD-74) had been authorized by the American Congress in March 1915, with construction taking place between 1916 and 1918.

The *Caldwell* class was designed as a multi-purpose platform to serve both as a battleship escort as well as a scouting ship. The armament array of all six of the *Caldwell*-class destroyers mirrored that of the *Sampson* class.

Trying Out New Designs

The original US Navy design plans for the *Caldwell* class envisioned a ship 310ft long with a displacement of 1,125 tons and an operational range of 2,500 miles. It was also intended to have three screws instead of the traditional two. Top speed was to be 30 knots. The original ship design also called for a submarine ram bow, although that feature did not appear on the production examples.

As events unfolded, the *Caldwell*-class destroyers became something of an experimental group with no two identical. Two of the six had the three-screw arrangement, with the other four retaining the more traditional two-screw arrangement.

The two *Caldwell*-class destroyers with the triple-screw arrangement also had an experimental powerplant configuration, whereas the other four had the now-standard steam turbine engines coupled to reduction gears as had first appeared on the USS *Wadsworth* (DD-60) of the *Tucker* class launched in 1915.

The two *Caldwell*-class vessels with the three-screw arrangement also only had three stacks rather than the four seen on the flivver and thousand-ton-type destroyers. The other four examples of the *Caldwell*-class destroyers that retained the traditional two-screw arrangement kept the one stack per boiler, of which the ship class had four.

Wickes-Class Destroyers

In 1916, Congress authorized construction of fifty new destroyers (DD-75 through to DD-124) referred to as the *Wickes* class. To save time, the Navy dispensed with designing a new type of destroyer from the ground up. Instead, the *Wickes*-class design was based on the four *Caldwell*-class destroyers fitted with the traditional two-screw arrangement and steam turbine engines coupled to reduction gears.

A problem developed as the *Caldwell* class was already nearing obsolescence when the decision was made to base the *Wickes* class on its design. Thus the US Navy would find itself badly lagging in destroyer designs compared to that of other nations, both during the First World War and during the interwar period.

At 314ft 4.5in, the *Wickes* class was a bit longer than the *Caldwell* class. Another eleven additional destroyers (DD-125 through to DD-135) of the *Wickes* class received authorization in May 1917. The president was authorized by Congress to order another fifteen *Wickes*-class destroyers (DD-136 through to DD-151) if he perceived the need, which he eventually did.

As the demand for destroyers continued to grow, another thirty-five examples were authorized and built (DD-152 through to DD-186). So great was the call for even more destroyers that new battleship and cruiser construction for the US Navy was put on hold so that shipyards could concentrate on the building of destroyers. In total, American shipyards completed 111 units of the *Wickes* class between 1917 and 1921.

Problems

Even before *Wickes*-class destroyers were commissioned, the US Navy uncovered a host of unforeseen design flaws during early trials. The ship's stern proved to be overly cramped, reducing the number of depth-charges that could be carried in stern racks. The placement of the four 4in deck guns also proved troublesome due to their restricted fields of fire.

The most severe design issue revolved around their range. The US Navy's contract specifications had called for a range of approximately 4,000 miles when cruising at 15 knots. The *Caldwell*-class destroyers built at one shipyard exceeded that specification, while those from another shipyard could only manage about 2,600 miles when sailing at the specified speed. It was this type of quality control problem that pushed the US Navy into seeking authorization from Congress for an improved class of destroyer.

Clemson-Class Destroyers

After a great deal of debate within the US Navy on the design of a suitable replacement for the troublesome *Wickes*-class destroyers, a modified version of the *Wickes* class was chosen to speed up production and became the *Clemson* class. Its envisioned role was to protect allied convoys and destroy German submarines when encountered.

With this in mind, the US Navy decided that the most crucial design feature was range. The US Navy wanted them to be able to steam approximately 4,600 miles on a single load of fuel. Thus they'd be capable of crossing the Atlantic at 15 knots. To accomplish this goal, they were to have larger fuel tanks than the previous *Caldwell* class.

Between 1918 and 1922 a total of 156 destroyers (DD-186 through to DD-347) of the *Clemson* class came out of American shipyards. The original US Navy plans had called for the construction of 162 examples, but the end of the First World War resulted in the cancellation of 6 of them. Displacement came in at 1,215 tons, with a length of 314ft 4.5in and a beam of 30ft 11.5in. Crew complement was 122 men.

Armament

The *Clemson* class had the same weapon array as the previous destroyers going back to the *Samson* class. With the US Navy becoming aware that a new type of German submarine was armed with 5.9in deck guns, it became concerned that the submarines would out-gun its destroyers in a surface battle. To rectify this problem, the US Navy had some of the decks strengthened on the *Clemson* class to mount larger and heavier 5in/51 (127mm) deck guns if needed. In the end, only five *Clemson*-class destroyers ever had such deck guns fitted.

Like the flivvers and the thousand-ton destroyers, the *Clemson* class was fitted with fantail depth-charge racks during the First World War; the depth-charges themselves merely rolled down the inclined metal racks and dropped off the ship's stern. To increase the breadth of a depth-charge pattern, the Royal Navy developed a projector that, with the detonation of an explosive propellant charge, would hurl a depth-charge to port or starboard to a certain safe distance.

Due to the recoil damage from these propellant charges to the ships' decks, the US Navy refined the design by using a recoilless compressed air system to hurl two depth-charges off the destroyers' sides at the same time in different directions. Due to its shape, the device became known as the 'Y-gun'. Y-gun production began for the US Navy in December 1918, too late for use in the First World War. However, they would see productive employment during the Second World War.

Unofficial Nicknames

The *Caldwell*-, *Wickes*- and *Clemson*-class destroyers acquired unofficial nicknames during their many years in service. These included 'flush-deckers', 'twelve-hundred-ton type', 'four-stackers' and 'four-pipers'. The first unofficial nickname referred to the straight main deck lines of the three destroyer classes and the second the relative displacement of the class.

In contrast, the earlier flivvers and thousand-ton types had a break in their deck lines behind their forecastles. The US Navy's definition of the forecastle is 'the upper deck forward of the foremast and included in the bow area.' A foremast is 'the first mast of a ship abaft [behind] the bow.'

The terms 'four-stackers' and 'four-pipers' referred to the four smokestacks on the *Caldwell*-, *Wickes*- and *Clemson*-class destroyers. However, the majority of previous US Navy destroyer classes also had four stacks yet had not received the same nicknames.

Service Use

Of the six *Caldwell*-class destroyers authorized for production, four were completed and commissioned before the end of the First World War and saw service during the conflict. Of the thirty-six examples of the *Wickes* class commissioned before the First World War ended, only half played any part in the conflict. A single *Clemson*-class destroyer entered into US Navy service several weeks after the war concluded.

None of the flush-deckers that did see service overseas accounted for any German submarines. However, in March 1918 two did attack an enemy submarine which managed to evade their best efforts to sink it. In July 1918, a flush-decker managed to drive off a German submarine attacking a merchant ship. Other flush-deckers aided in rescuing civilian crews of merchant ships sunk by German U-boats.

Post-First World War

Instead of cancelling construction of a large number of *Wickes*- and *Clemson*-class destroyers following the First World War, the US Navy allowed the contracts to continue. This led to a massive glut of surplus destroyers built between 1919 and 1921. The majority of the completed destroyers went directly into the US Navy's reserve fleet. Those that remained in active service did so with skeleton crews.

Six of the flush-deckers went to the US Coast Guard to take part in the Rum Patrols between 1920 and 1933. With the end of Prohibition, the loaned-out flush-deckers returned to the US Navy inventory to be decommissioned and scrapped.

Due to their age and treaty obligations, a number of the *Wickes*- and *Clemson*-class destroyers were eventually decommissioned and sold for scrap in the 1930s. By 1936, only 169 examples of the *Caldwell*-, *Wickes*- and *Clemson*-class destroyers remained, most in the reserve fleet.

Prior to the Second World War

The US Navy was more than aware of the obsolete nature of its stockpile of flush-deckers following the First World War. However, requests for funding to modernize the vessels during the 1920s and most of the 1930s never came to fruition.

As the Axis Powers, Germany and Italy, continued on an even more belligerent and aggressive path overseas during the late 1930s with Japan joining them in mid-1940, the US Navy realized that it would soon be forced to confront the Axis Powers militarily. At the end of 1940, with sufficient funding now available, the Navy began a programme to recommission and modernize a portion of its decommissioned flush-deckers.

A total of thirty-seven flush-deckers were modernized before the Japanese attack at Pearl Harbor on 7 December 1941. At that point the programme ended, as the US Navy wanted available funding devoted to construction of new classes of much more modern destroyers as Congress became much more amenable to paying for them.

In the autumn of 1941, the US Navy had 119 flush-deckers in active service with 71 in the destroyer role and 48 others serving in a variety of other jobs. Most of those serving as destroyers found themselves classified at the time as second-line ships.

Into Combat

Even before the Japanese attack at Pearl Harbor several incidents occurred in the Atlantic between flush-deckers of President Franklin D. Roosevelt's organized 'Neutrality Patrol' and German submarines. One of those incidents resulted in the sinking of the flush-decker USS *Reuben James* (DD-245) in October 1941, with the loss of 115 members of her 160-man crew.

It was another flush-decker, the USS *Ward* (DD-139), that engaged and sank a Japanese mini-submarine at the entrance to Pearl Harbor on 7 December 1941 before Japanese carrier aircraft attacked. Until the next generation of destroyers came out of the shipyards in sufficient numbers, those flush-deckers still on active duty with the US Navy would have to hold the line in both the Pacific and the Atlantic.

There were thirteen US Navy flush-deckers in the Far East when the Japanese attacked Pearl Harbor. During the weeks that followed, four would be sunk by the Japanese. The last flush-decker in the destroyer role would be pulled from the Pacific in March 1941 as their short range and inadequate anti-aircraft weaponry made them far too vulnerable to enemy aircraft.

Flush-deckers would remain in front-line service as destroyers in the Atlantic between 1942 and 1943, primarily as convoy escorts. Their lack of anti-aircraft weapons proved not to be a hindrance as enemy submarines remained the primary threat, not enemy aircraft. To improve the *Wickes*-class destroyers' range, most still in service had one of their four boilers removed and replaced by an extra fuel tank.

Besides convoy escort duties, flush-deckers took an active role in going after German submarines along with US Navy escort carriers as part of what became known as 'hunter-killer groups'. In total six German submarines were sunk by flush-deckers during the Second World War. In addition to the USS *Reuben James* (DD-245) sunk before the United States' official entry into the war, German submarines accounted for three other US Navy flush-deckers during the conflict.

End of the Line

As American shipyards began to produce large numbers of next-generation destroyers, the remaining flush-deckers serving as destroyers were themselves pushed into less demanding secondary roles such as training ships, or were just pulled from service.

Two days after the Japanese surrender on 2 September 1945 that brought an end to the Second World War, the US Navy had only seventy-six flush-deckers in service.

Of that number only four were still classified as destroyers; the US Navy had converted the others into several variants. With the end of the war, the US Navy began decommissioning the remaining flush-deckers, with the last going off to the scrapyards in 1947.

Flush-Decker Variants

With an excess of flush-deckers post-First World War, the US Navy began considering employing some of them for secondary duties. Eventually, ninety went to the shipyards for conversion between 1919 and 1944. This proved to be a much more cost-effective option for the US Navy than spending available funding on new ships to serve in those roles.

The first new role for the flush-deckers began in 1919; two were converted into seaplane tenders in a test programme that lasted until 1922. After that, interest in the seaplane tender role waned until 1939, and in 1940 the programme began once again as America saw itself eventually drawn into the Second World War.

By the time of the Japanese attack on Pearl Harbor, the US Navy had fourteen flush-decker-based seaplane tenders in the fleet. All would see service during the conflict. With the wartime construction of new specially-designed seaplane tenders, only four of the flush-deckers remained as seaplane tenders when the Second World War ended. The other ten examples found themselves converted for different roles and eventually scrapped after the war.

Foreign Flush-Deckers

To aid the then hard-pressed British, in September 1940 President Franklin D. Roosevelt arranged for the transfer of fifty flush-deckers from the US Navy's reserve fleet to the Royal Navy. In exchange, the American military was allowed to build bases at various British overseas possessions such as Newfoundland and the British West Indies.

Such was the poor condition of the flush-deckers that came out of the US Navy's reserve fleet that the Royal Navy found just thirty sufficiently fit for use on delivery. The Royal Navy lost nine of them to various causes during the Second World War. They would go on to scrap their last remaining examples in 1949. Late in the war the Royal Navy lent the Red Navy nine flush-deckers. All returned, the last in 1952, and they were quickly scrapped.

A single example of a scuttled US Navy flush-decker, left in dry dock in the Philippines in early 1942, would be rebuilt by the Japanese Navy and placed into service. Captured by the US Navy at the end of the Second World War, it would be towed back to the United States' West Coast and later sunk as a target during a training exercise.

Mine Warfare Destroyers

The Royal Navy had made successful use of mine-layers during the First World, prompting the US Navy to convert fourteen flush-deckers into mine-layers in 1920. Their number would vary during the interwar period, with those reaching the end of their service life being decommissioned and replaced by others from the reserve fleet. By the time the United States entered the Second World War, the US Navy had eight flush-decker mine-layers in the fleet, losing two during the conflict.

Another equally important role assigned to modified flush-deckers would be mine-sweeping. The Navy had first tested the concept on a flush-decker in 1935 but did not embrace the role until 1940 when eight flush-deckers went into the shipyards for conversion. Pleased with the result, the US Navy had ten more converted in 1940.

During the Second World War, five of the flush-decker mine-sweepers went down. Mid-war, newer classes of converted destroyers took over the role of mine-sweepers. Those flush-deckers modified for the mine-sweeper role that survived the war quickly went to the scrapyards.

Fast Troop Transports

With the interwar anticipation of a future war with Japan, the US Navy foresaw a requirement for a high-speed troop transport for moving Marine Raiders around the Pacific from island to island. Rather than going through the time-consuming process of designing and building a new specialized vessel for that role, the Navy decided that flush-deckers could rather easily be converted for the new job which resulted in a prototype in 1939, APD-1, and thirty-two additional examples completed between 1940 and 1944.

Like the flush-deckers converted into seaplane tenders, those converted into high-speed troop transports would eventually see themselves replaced during the war by newer ships. Some, however, remained in service until the end of the war towing targets or as training vessels. The job of high-speed troop transport was not without its dangers: nine went down during the war. With the war's end, all the remaining examples went to the scrapyards.

(**Opposite, above**) The USS *Cushing* (TB-1) pictured here entered US Navy service in April 1890. The US Congress authorized its construction in August 1866, shortly after the American Civil War. With a crew of twenty-two, it would be the US Navy's first production torpedo boat. Five experimental torpedo boats – the *Lightning*, *Destroyer*, *Alarm*, *Intrepid* and *Stiletto* – were built and tested before the USS *Cushing*'s introduction into service. (*Navy Historical Center*, hereafter *NHC*)

(**Opposite, below**) Powered by two vertical quadruple-expansion reciprocating steam engines, the USS *Cushing* (TB-1) had a maximum speed of 23 knots. The ship is seen here on a period postcard. The US Navy had wanted a top speed of 26 knots, but existing maritime technology was not up to the task. USS *Cushing*'s armament consisted of three torpedo tubes. (*NHC*)

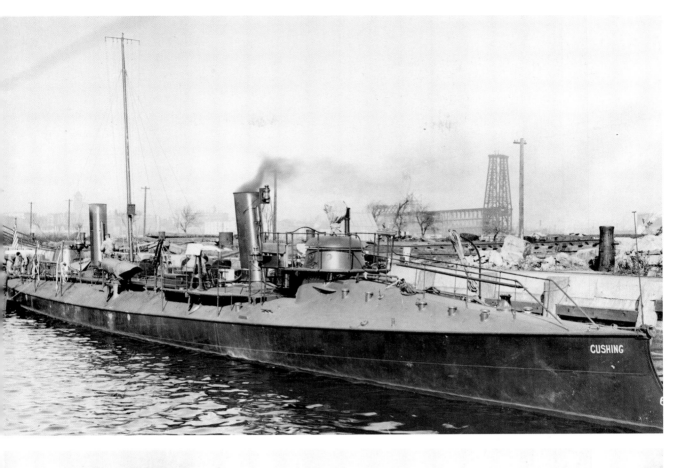

Torpedo Boat Cushing, 22.5 Knots.

Berthed together are two of the thirty-five production torpedo boats commissioned by the US Navy between 1890 and 1904. USS *Ericsson* (TB-2, pictured) was authorized for construction in July 1890, but not completed and commissioned until February 1897 due to the inexperience of the firm commissioned to build her. Her decommissioning took place in April 1912. (*NHC*)

Pictured here is a 3-pounder (47mm) Mk 15 deck gun on a pedestal mount. The pedestal is fixed to the ship's deck, and the weapon was manually traversed, elevated and depressed. Having entered into US Navy service in the late 1880s, the weapon armed many of the thirty-five torpedo boats. It also appeared on many of the US Navy's cruisers and battleships as an anti-torpedo-boat weapon. (NHC)

Shown during its fitting-out is the USS *Thornton* (TB-33). The ship was one of nine torpedo boats belonging to the *Blakeley* class, the last and largest class of the torpedo boats. Commissioned in June 1902, the twenty-eight-man ship had three pedestal-mounted 3-pounder (47mm) Mk 15 guns and three torpedo tubes. Maximum speed topped out at 25 knots. (NHC)

TORPEDO BOAT NO. 33

U. S. S. THORNTON

JUNE 30 1900

U S S Barry 302-5

(**Opposite, above**) To counter other navies' use of torpedo boats, the US Navy embraced the concept of 'torpedo boat destroyers'. Pictured here is the USS *Whipple* (TBD-15), one of sixteen torpedo-boat destroyers of the *Bainbridge* class, built for the US Navy between 1899 and 1903. The vessel's bulbous forecastle is a 'turtle-back'. In the 1920s torpedo-boat destroyers were renamed 'destroyers' by the US Navy. *(NHC)*

(**Above**) The seventy-three officers and enlisted men of USS *Bainbridge*, the US Navy's first destroyer, appear in this picture. In the front row are the ship's officers and on the far left in the second row can be seen the vessel's two mess stewards. Typical of the time, the ship's bridge was completely open, with the canvas awning in the photograph as the only protection from the elements. As the ship was intended as a coastal vessel only, this design feature would not be as serious an issue as envisioned. *(NHC)*

(**Opposite, below**) The USS *Barry* (DD-2) pictured here had her commissioning in November 1902. She lacked the bulbous forecastle of other *Bainbridge*-class destroyers. Instead, she had a raised forecastle at the bow. The US Navy definition of a forecastle: 'A short structure at the forward end of a vessel formed by carrying up the ship's shell plating a deck height above the level of her uppermost complete deck and fitting a deck over the length of this structure.' *(NHC)*

On the evening of 26 August 1918, while steaming in a dense fog near the port of Brest, France, the *Bainbridge*-class USS *Stewart* (DD-13) was rammed by an unidentified civilian ship. The resulting damage is evident in this photograph. During the First World War, USS *Stewart* attacked two German submarines but failed to destroy them. *(NHC)*

At an American shipyard is a coal-fired boiler ready for installation in a *Bainbridge*-class destroyer. The ships' coal-fired boilers supplied high-pressure steam to their triple-expansion reciprocating steam engines. The first successful maritime application of a triple-expansion reciprocating steam engine occurred in 1881, with the launching of a British cargo ship named the *Aberdeen*. (*NHC*)

Two vertical triple-expansion reciprocating steam engines intended for a US Navy cruiser. A continuing issue that would divide the senior ranks of the US Navy during the early history of destroyers would be speed. Many wanted the destroyers to possess the highest speeds possible, while others cautioned that high speed in a destroyer meant nothing if the engines that propelled it were not reliable. (*NHC*)

(**Opposite, above**) The size difference between the US Navy's very early destroyers and its torpedo boats is evident in this image. On the far left is the USS *Lawrence* (TBD-8) commissioned in April 1903. It had a length of 246ft 3in. To her right are the USS *Farragut* (TB-11) with a length of 214ft and the USS *Goldsborough* (TB-20) with a length of 198ft. (*NHC*)

(**Above**) Pictured on a US Navy destroyer during a training exercise is a pedestal-mounted 57mm Mk 15 deck gun. At the time it was referred to as a '6-pounder', a British ordnance rating system dating from 1764 that classified a gun by the weight of its round and not its bore diameter. The *Bainbridge* class had six 57mm Mk 15 deck guns. (*NHC*)

(**Opposite, below**) The USS *Flusser* (TBD-20) shown here was one of five ships in the *Smith* class (TBD-17 to TBD-21) built between 1908 and 1910. With the advent of the *Smith* class, the turtle-back forecastle that first appeared on the US Navy's torpedo boats and some of the *Bainbridge*-class destroyers disappeared as a design feature. (*NHC*)

In this 1914 photograph, we see one turbine's shaft and blades removed from a destroyer. A steam turbine engine is a rotary engine consisting of curved blades mounted on a shaft. The curved blades turn in response to high-pressure steam impinging on them, which in turn converts the thermal energy to mechanical energy. The turbine shafts transfer the mechanical energy to a reduction gear, which gears down the turbine shaft's rotation to turn a propeller shaft at a slower speed but higher (shaft) horsepower. (*NHC*)

(**Opposite**) In the engine room of a *Smith*-class destroyer, we are looking forward at the control board. The *Smith*-class ships had steam turbine engines instead of the triple-expansion reciprocating steam engines of the *Bainbridge*-class destroyers. The former became standard on all subsequent destroyer classes until the 1960s. In the second lower picture we are looking aft. In the background are two of the ship's four coal-fired boilers that provided high-pressure steam to three steam turbine engines that in turn rotated three propeller shafts. Maximum speed of the *Smith* class was 28 knots. (*NHC*)

The largest deck gun on the *Bainbridge* class and *Smith* class was the 3in/50, with an example pictured here on a pedestal mount aboard a non-destroyer. The original version of the gun appeared in 1898 and was intended for engaging only surface targets. With a muzzle velocity of 2,100 feet per second, the early models of the gun had a maximum range of 7,000 yards. (*NHC*)

Shown here is one of the three single torpedo-tube launchers on a *Smith*-class torpedo-boat destroyer armed with an 18in-diameter torpedo. British engineer Robert Whitehead invented the first self-propelled torpedo in 1866. Initially the US Navy used various licence-built models of the Whitehead torpedo until 1904, when it switched to the American-designed and built Bliss-Leavitt torpedo series. (*NHC*)

Pictured here is an example of the Bliss-Leavitt torpedo labelled the Mk 7 that entered into US Navy service in 1912. The 18in-diameter torpedo armed both destroyers and submarines. With a length of 17ft, it weighed 1,628lb and had a high-explosive warhead of 326lb. At a speed of 35 knots, it had a maximum range of 6,000 yards. *(NHC)*

The USS *McCall* (TBD-28) seen in this picture was one of twenty-one *Pauling*-class destroyers (TBD-22 through to TBD-42) built between 1908 and 1917. They were the first to have oil-fired boilers instead of coal-fired boilers to drive their steam turbines. The US Navy officially switched to oil in 1904. *(NHC)*

(**Above**) In dry dock here is the USS *Warrington* (TBD-30), a *Pauling*-class destroyer commissioned in March 1911. Like the *Smith* class, the *Pauling* class had as its main armament five of the pedestal-mounted 3in/50 deck guns. As already mentioned, in the 1920s the US Navy shortened the label 'torpedo-boat destroyer' to simply 'destroyer' and assigned them all the letter prefix 'DD'. (*NHC*)

(**Opposite, above**) On 22 July 1918, the *Pauling*-class destroyer the USS *Jarvis* (DD-38) collided with another US Navy destroyer off the French coast and lost most of her bow. Here we see the ship with temporary repairs made so she could sail for England to have a new bow fitted. Repairs on the *Jarvis* were finished in September 1918. (*NHC*)

(**Opposite, below**) Visible on the stern of the USS *Fanning* (DD-37), a *Pauling*-class destroyer, is a large number of depth-charges divided between two racks. On 17 November 1917, the *Fanning* and another destroyer depth-charged and badly damaged a submerged German submarine, forcing it to surface. Once on the surface, the submarine's crew surrendered and were taken aboard the *Fanning* before their vessel sank. (*NHC*)

On the *Pauling*-class destroyers appeared the first twin 18in-diameter torpedo tubes as pictured here. Each ship had four such mounts, two on either side of the ship's main deck, that had only limited traverse. Aiming and firing was performed by the sailor seen here on the top of the torpedo tube mount. *(NHC)*

A First World War addition to many US Navy destroyers that served overseas was the British-invented Y-gun seen here. The US Navy assigned it the designation Depth Charge Projector Mk I. Built of grey cast iron, the weapon weighed 1,250lb. The barrels connected to a spherical powder chamber. The weapon had a range of 50 yards to either side of a ship. (NHC)

Following the twenty-one destroyers of the *Pauling* class, the US Navy built four *Cassin*-class destroyers (DD-43 through to DD-46) between 1912 and 1915. They were the first destroyer class nicknamed 'thousand tonners' due to their displacement. The previous destroyer classes received the nickname of 'flivvers' as they reminded sailors of the cheap rickety cars of the day. (NHC)

The four *Cassin*-class destroyers were the first to feature the pedestal-mounted 4in/50 deck gun with an example pictured here. It was the replacement for the pedestal-mounted 3in/50 deck guns on all earlier destroyer classes. Whereas the *Smith*- and *Pauling*-class destroyers had five of the pedestal-mounted 3in/50 as their main battery, the *Cassin* class main battery consisted of only four of the pedestal-mounted 4in/50 guns. (*NHC*)

One of the four *Cassin*-class destroyers in 1917 had its four single-mount 4in/50 deck guns replaced by four twin-mount 4in/50 deck guns as seen in this photograph. For whatever reason, the experiment proved a failure and the ship soon reverted to four single-mount 4in/50 deck guns. One might assume that the weight and the guns' recoil proved to be a problem. (*NHC*)

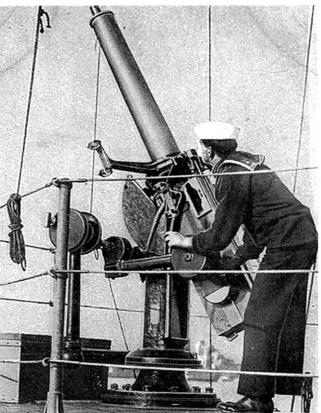

The only anti-aircraft gun available to US Navy destroyers before the First World War was the pedestal-mounted 1-pounder (37mm gun) Mk 6 seen here on an old postcard. Merely a scaled-up Maxim machine gun, the weapon appeared in US Navy service shortly before the Spanish-American War. It had the popular nickname of the 'pom-pom' due to the sound it made when firing. (*NHC*)

(**Above**) Next in line after authorization of the four *Cassin*-class destroyers were four near-identical repeats referred to as the *Aylwin* class (DD-47 through to DD-50). During the First World War, the *Aylwin* and other destroyer classes were fitted with the pedestal-mounted 3in/23 anti-aircraft gun as pictured here. A well-trained crew could fire between eight and nine rounds per minute to an altitude of 18,000ft. (*NHC*)

(**Opposite, above**) Between 1913 and 1915, American shipyards built six destroyers of the *O'Brien* class (DD-51 through to DD-56) with the USS *McDougal* (DD-54) shown here. The *O'Brien* class was an improved version of the previous *Aylwin* class. Rather than the 18in-diameter torpedoes of earlier destroyer classes, the *O'Brien* class had the new 21in-diameter torpedoes labelled the Bliss-Leavitt Mk 8. (*NHC*)

(**Opposite, below**) A prototype of a 21in-diameter torpedo in 1909. The 21in-diameter Bliss-Leavitt Mk 8 torpedo, with a 466lb high-explosive warhead, entered US Navy service in 1911. In 1926, the Mk 11 21in-diameter torpedo appeared, only to be replaced by the more reliable Mk 12 21in-diameter torpedo in 1928. Both had 500lb high-explosive warheads. (*NHC*)

(**Opposite, above**) In a First World War dazzle camouflage paint scheme is the USS *Wadsworth* (DD-60), one of six *Tucker*-class destroyers (DD-57 through to DD-62) built for the US Navy between 1914 and 1916. All six would see service during the First World War, with one sunk by a German submarine in December 1917. The remaining ships continued in US Navy service until 1922. (*NHC*)

(**Opposite, below**) On 9 October 1918, the rudder jammed on the USS *Shaw* (DD-68), a *Sampson*-class destroyer, one of six built between 1915 and 1916 (DD-63 through to DD-68). As the ship could no longer manoeuvre, she collided with a merchant ship that cut off 90ft of her bow and crushed her bridge. Twelve men died in the collision, but the ship remained afloat. Pictured here is an artist's view of some of the *Shaw*'s crew in the water after the collision. (*NHC*)

(**Above**) The *Sampson* class was the last of the so-called thousand-ton destroyers. They retained the main gun battery of four pedestal-mounted 4in/50 deck guns as had first appeared on the *Cassin* class and the three following destroyer classes. The major armament difference was the addition of four new three-tube torpedo-firing mounts, with an example pictured here on a US Navy cruiser's main deck. (*NHC*)

(**Opposite, above**) The USS *Caldwell* (DD-69) pictured here was the first of the five ships of the *Caldwell* class (DD-69 through to DD-74) built for the US Navy between 1916 and 1920. Considered experimental prototypes, no two were exactly alike. They were to help the US Navy identify what they wanted in the next class of destroyers. (*NHC*)

(**Above**) With America's official entry into the First World War in April 1917, the US Navy saw the need for a lot of destroyers in a hurry. To expedite matters, the decision came about to mass-produce a modified version of the *Caldwell* class. A key external design feature of the *Caldwell* class and the two follow-on destroyer classes was their flush-deck design, as is apparent in this photograph of the USS *Evans* (DD-78), a *Wickes*-class destroyer. (*NHC*)

(**Opposite, below**) The US Navy contracted with ten different shipyards to eventually construct a total of 111 examples of the *Wickes*-class destroyers, starting with the USS *Wickes* (DD-75) and ending with the USS *Bagley* (DD-185) between 1917 and 1921. Pictured here is the USS *Calhoun* (DD-85) during the First World War. Popular nicknames for the class were 'four-stackers', 'four-pipers' and 'flush-deckers'. (*NHC*)

(**Opposite, above**) An impressive image of a large number of oil-fired boilers for fitting out either the *Wickes*-class or follow-on *Clemson*-class destroyers. Boilers take in feedwater that circulates through pipes within. When a sailor lights a boiler, the combustion of fuel oil converts chemical energy to thermal energy which transforms feedwater into high-pressure steam that transfers the thermal energy into mechanical energy as it drives the turbines' shafts and the propeller shafts. (*NHC*)

(**Opposite, below**) The two triple torpedo-firing mounts on the port side of the USS *Blakeley* (DD-150), a *Wickes*-class destroyer, are seen here during a training exercise in the 1920s. The triple torpedo tubes had first appeared on the *Sampson* class. In a 1940 modernization programme, twenty-seven examples of the flush-deck destroyers had their two aft triple torpedo tubes removed in favour of additional anti-aircraft guns. (*NHC*)

(**Above**) The USS *Decatur* (DD-341) seen here passing through the Panama Canal sometime in the 1920s or 1930s belonged to the *Clemson* class of 156 destroyers. Built between 1918 and 1922, they were a modified version of the *Wickes* class that unfortunately were obsolete when constructed when compared to the destroyers then being put into service by other major navies. (*NHC*)

(**Opposite, above**) There was a concern early on with the *Clemson*-class design that larger enemy submarine deck guns might outgun them. In response, five of the 156 built had the 5in/51 deck gun installed, with an example pictured here, in place of their standard 4in/50 deck guns. However, as the threat proved overblown, the majority went to sea with the original 4in/50 deck guns. (*Vladimir Yakubov*)

(**Opposite, below**) Seen here during under-way refuelling is the pre-Second World War USS *Pruitt* (DD-347) of the *Clemson* class. The ship was the last of the flush-deck destroyers built. Commissioned in June 1920, the ship went through a process that changed her role to that of a mine-layer in 1937. The ship was re-designated DM-22. (*NHC*)

(**Above**) Taking part in a pre-Second World War training exercise are three flush-deck destroyers: in the foreground is the USS *Long* (DD-209), with the USS *James K. Paulding* (DD-238) in the background. Both ships were *Clemson*-class destroyers. The pole mast behind each ship's bridge is in the US Navy referred to as the foremast, and the one at the stern of the ship as the main mast. (*NHC*)

On the night of 8 September 1923, thirteen flush-deck destroyers were taking part in a training exercise along the Central California coast. Through a series of human errors compounded by fog and strong currents, seven of the thirteen ran aground at a location known as Honda Point. Four ships – USS *Chauncey* (DD-296), USS *Young* (DD-312, capsized aft of *Chauncey*), SS *Woodbury* (DD-309) and USS *Fuller* (DD-297, mast behind the rocks) – appear in this photograph. Pounding waves would eventually destroy all those grounded. (*NHC*)

Chapter Two

Interwar Destroyers

In spite of the US Navy's pressing requirement for more modern destroyers, it took until September 1932 before construction began on the eight ships of the *Farragut* class (DD-328 through to DD-335), the US Navy's first post-First World War class of destroyers. They came out of the shipyards between 1932 and 1935. The entire class went on to see service during the Second World War with three lost due to non-combat events: two in a typhoon and one that ran aground.

The *Farragut* class's initial crew complement of 160 men rose to 250 during the Second World War. This wartime increase was mirrored on all the other pre-Second World War destroyer classes. One of the reasons was the addition of a large number of labour-intensive anti-aircraft guns.

Description

With a length of 341ft 3in and a beam of 34ft 3in, the *Farragut* class was larger than its flush-decker predecessors and differed externally a great deal from the flush-deckers. Whereas the flush-deckers had four stacks, the *Farragut* had only two.

Rather than having the flush-decker's straight main deck lines, the *Farragut* class reverted to raised forecastles to improve seakeeping, a design feature seen on the flivvers and thousand-ton destroyers.

The propulsion plant consisted of four fuel-oil boilers and two steam turbine engines coupled to single reduction gears, the same as the flush-deckers. The *Farragut* class also retained the flush-deckers' two-propeller arrangement, as did all following destroyer classes.

To improve endurance, economizers were added to the propulsion plant. The economizers scavenged energy from stack gasses and used it to pre-heat the distilled feedwater being fed into the ship's four boilers; the boilers in turn superheated the steam.

Superheating steam increases thermal energy. The increased efficiency reduces the amount of fuel oil required to generate each pound of steam, creating size and weight savings throughout a ship's propulsion plant. The *Farragut* class was the US Navy's first with boilers capable of generating superheated steam, a design feature on all sub-sequent destroyer classes.

Armament

The *Farragut* class featured five new dual-purpose 5in/38 guns suitable for engaging both surface and aerial targets (dual-purpose). The two 5in/38 guns forward of the ship's bridge had partially-enclosed mounts. The three 5in/38 guns located aft of the ship's superstructure were open mounts, as a weight-saving measure.

From a 1945 US Navy manual is this passage describing a gun mount:

> Every gun mounting, whatever its size, is, in essence, a strongly-built turntable, upon which is fitted a pair of brackets adapted to receive the trunnions of the cradle and so carry the gun. The turntable enables the gun to be trained round to any desired direction, and the trunnion pins and brackets form a pivot about which it can be elevated or depressed as required.

The *Farragut* class pre-war anti-aircraft armament consisted of four .50-calibre (12.7mm) machine guns. Combat experience during the Second World War proved this to be wholly inadequate, so the machine guns were replaced by a larger number of immediate-range 40mm and short-range 20mm anti-aircraft guns. To improve the 5in guns' accuracy, each ship of the *Farragut* class had a 'gun director'.

There was also a manually-operated gun director for the 40mm anti-aircraft guns designated the Mk 51. An improved power-operated version referred to as the Mk 49 appeared later in the war. When their director went down, the 40mm anti-aircraft gun crews employed tracer fire or used metal sights with concentric rings to engage targets. The 20mm anti-aircraft guns were manually aimed, and eventually fitted with an automatic lead-computing sight designated the Mk 14, the Mk 15 and finally the Mk 20.

The torpedo count on the *Farragut*'s class came to eight, split between two quadruple torpedo-launching mounts ('quad mounts') on raised platforms along the centreline of the ships. They could be trained through a wide arc and fired over either side of the ship. A black powder impulse charge expelled the 21in-diameter torpedoes with enough force to clear the ship's main deck.

For the ASW role, the *Farragut* class was fitted with two stern roll-off depth-charge racks like those on the flush-deckers. They would also have four 'K-gun' depth-charge projectors introduced into service in 1941. A 1943 US Navy manual on the K-gun

---

Enclosed Mount versus Turret

In the US Navy nomenclature system, 'enclosed mounts' are unarmoured mounts offering only protection from the elements, splinter protection and muzzle blast. If classified as a 'turret', in the US Navy nomenclature system, then a gun mount is armoured. Turrets were found on US Navy cruisers and battleships. As a generalization, enclosed mounts are technically turrets.

Gun Directors

Though manual operation by gun crews was possible, the primary method for controlling the *Farragut*'s dual-purpose main guns was the Mk 33 gun director. The director was enclosed within a weaponless open mount on top of the ship's forward superstructure directly above the bridge. Later model gun directors, such as the Mk 37, were fitted to destroyers in enclosed mounts.

Early versions of the gun directors were manually traversed (trained); later models were powered. Their crews employed a telescope and optical stereo range-finder to determine the bearing to a target as well as elevation and range. Following models had radar added, which greatly increased their capabilities, especially for firing at night and in inclement weather (fog and rain).

An essential feature in the functioning of a gun director was a stable element. It measured the angle of the deck from horizontal as the ship rolled (port and starboard) and pitched (fore and aft).

To develop a fire-control solution for a destroyer's guns, the information obtained by the gun director went to an analogue electromechanical computer located within the ship. The computer accepted all ballistic factors as well as data on its own ship course and speed. It, in turn, transmitted gun position data to the powered-operated gun mounts it oversaw. The gun crew then positioned the weapon manually or under power based on the firing solution provided.

The actual firing of the guns would typically be done by the gun director crew or from a plotting room (plot) located within a ship. Upon firing, the gun director crews would both observe and make corrections if a target remained unscathed.

There could be any number of variables in the initial firing data to account for a missed target. External ballistic factors such as wind could also contribute to projectiles missing their intended destination. When this occurred, additional firing data had to be obtained based on where the initial hits landed in relation to the target. Further salvos were then fired until target destruction was ensured.

describes its role: 'The primary purpose of these weapons is to project depth-charges to port and starboard of vessels in order to enlarge and supplement the pattern obtained by [the depth] charges dropped from the stern.'

Treaty-Class Destroyers

Displacement of the *Farragut* class was approximately 1,365 tons. The maximum displacement of the class was set at 1,500 tons during its design phase by the provisions of the London Naval Treaty of 1930. The United States government had been a signatory to the treaty in the vain hope that the treaty would aid in preventing a costly arms race among the major naval powers of the day.

Besides the eight *Farragut*-class destroyers, the US Navy received funding for another four classes of very similar but not identical destroyers; all were roughly within the 1,500-ton displacement treaty limits. The forty destroyers of the *Mahan*, *Gridley*, *Bagley* and *Benham* classes were completed by 1939.

The most numerous would be the eighteen examples of the *Mahan* class, followed by the ten destroyers of the *Benham* class. Eight examples of the *Bagley* class and four of the *Gridley* class rounded out the construction. The DD numbers for the forty-eight vessels of the 1,500-ton displacement destroyers built were not in sequential order.

The *Benham* Class

Reflecting a continuous series of improvements during the period in which the 1,500-ton displacement destroyer classes were in production the last class, the *Benham*, built between 1936 and 1939, while overall very similar to the first class, the *Farragut*, had some differences internally and externally.

The main external spotting feature for the *Benham* class (DD-397 through to DD-399 and DD-402 through to DD-408) was its single stack, whereas all the other previous 1,500-ton displacement destroyer classes had two. The deck space not needed for the second stack was available for additional equipment.

Engineering

Internally, the *Benham* class had only three boilers instead of the four on all previous destroyer classes. The reduction was made possible by the interwar development of high-strength steel alloys in the boiler construction that improved both their strength and heat-resisting qualities. In turn the configuration had greater power output and higher efficiency in the *Benham* class as well as follow-on destroyer classes.

The two steam turbine engines of the *Benham* class were coupled to double reduction gears rather than single reduction gears. The latter had first appeared on the *Mahan*-class destroyers of the 1,500-ton displacement classes (DD-364 through to DD-378 and DD-384 through to DD-385).

Top speed for the *Benham* class came to 37.9 knots. Cruising turbines, optimized for minimal fuel consumption at a moderate speed to extend its endurance, supplemented the steam turbine engines. The ship's range came out to 6,200 statute miles.

Destroyer Displacements

All the interwar destroyer classes except the first, the *Farragut* class, proved overweight as they exceeded the treaty limitations (more by accident than by intent). Despite their actual commissioning weight, they were always referred to as 1,500-ton displacement destroyers.

Benham-*Class Armament*

The *Benham* class had only four single-mount 5in/38 dual-purpose guns instead of the five of the *Farragut* class to leave room for a torpedo-firing mount. Where the *Farragut* class had two centreline-mounted quad mounts that could fire to either side, the *Benham*-class ships had four torpedo quad mounts – two on either side of the ship's main deck – only capable of firing to one side.

Like all the pre-Second World War destroyer classes, the *Benham* class had its original pre-war anti-aircraft armament eventually replaced with 40mm and 20mm anti-aircraft guns. Also, some of the *Benham* class had both K-guns and even the older-generation Y-guns installed to supplement their two stern depth-charge racks.

As the threat from aircraft increased during the war and the chance of employing torpedoes against enemy warships diminished, some of the *Benham* class had

---

Torpedo Issues

The effectiveness of US Navy 21in-diameter torpedoes carried by destroyers early in the war would be a serious issue due to design flaws with the weapon. An example of this issue appears in the following passage from a Naval Historical Center publication regarding the Battle of Santa Cruz Islands on 26 October 1942, when the destroyer USS *Mustin* was called upon to sink the abandoned aircraft carrier USS *Hornet* (CV-8) to prevent her falling into enemy hands:

> At 1903 the *Mustin*'s [DD-413] torpedo batteries went into action. All eight Mark 15 Model 1 torpedoes equipped with Mark 6 Model 1 exploders were fired with 'most discouraging results', according to the action report: 'Torpedoes were fired singly at a range of 2,000 to 3,000 yards with a cold set-up and missing the point of aim was impossible. The depth was set at 26 feet for the first three torpedoes, at 10 feet for the next four, and at 15 for the last torpedo. Torpedo speed was set at intermediate for the first five shots and at low speed for the last three. All torpedo tracks were observed for some time after leaving the ship in the dusk, and all appeared to be running hot, straight and normal. No evidence whatsoever of any explosion could be observed with either the first or last torpedo. The second torpedo reappeared several minutes after having been fired, leaping into the air about 300 yards broad on the [*Mustin*'s] starboard quarter and exploding violently, showering the ship with fragments … A third torpedo did not explode but was observed broaching wildly astern of the carrier on a course approximately at right angles to that at which it was fired … Sometime after the fourth torpedo was fired a dull explosion was heard, and it is suspected that this torpedo functioned, although no evidence could be noted on the target. The fifth, sixth and seventh torpedoes apparently hit and functioned normally.

their torpedo-launching mounts reduced in number or removed entirely in favour of additional 40mm and 20mm anti-aircraft guns.

In US Navy documents the 40mm anti-aircraft guns on destroyers are also referred to as the 'heavy machine gun battery' and the 20mm anti-aircraft guns as the 'light machine gun battery'. In some reports only the label 'machine guns' appears.

Before the Second World War the *Benham* class had a crew complement of 184 men. In wartime, the crew size rose to approximately 251 men. Two ships of the class were lost in combat, both to enemy torpedoes: one in the Pacific from the Japanese, and one in the Atlantic from the Germans.

Larger Treaty Destroyers

Following on the heels of the first *Farragut*-class destroyers there came eight destroyers of the *Porter* class (DD-356 through to DD-363) built between 1933 and 1937. The *Porter* class was not bound by the London Naval Treaty of 1930, which limited maximum displacement to 1,500 tons. Instead, they fell under a provision in the same treaty allowing the US Navy to build thirteen destroyers with a maximum displacement of 1,850 tons.

The *Porter* class had a length of 381ft and a beam of 36ft 2in. A crew of 206 men staffed them before the Second World War, growing to a total of 290 men during the conflict. Pushing the US Navy into acquiring the *Porter* class was the awareness that other major navies, such as the Japanese and French, were building ever larger and more capable destroyers during the interwar period.

The main propulsion plant arrangement on the *Porter* class was generally the same as that of the *Farragut* class. The maximum range came out at 7,340 miles with the two steam turbine engines coupled to single reduction gears. The *Porter* class had no cruising turbines.

Envisioned Roles

Due to their larger size, the *Porter* class initially were classified as 'destroyer leaders', a somewhat obsolete term by the late 1930s. The original concept evolved with the British Royal Navy before the First World War when a small number of larger destroyers, named 'flotilla leaders', acted as 'command and control' vessels for groups of smaller destroyers. By the 1930s, US Navy destroyers had a more than capable communications set-up that did away with the need for destroyer leaders.

Besides the envisioned role as destroyer leaders, the US Navy leadership also believed that the yet-to-be-built *Porter* class could fill in for its lack of sufficient numbers of light cruisers. Light cruisers at the time were typically employed in the scouting role by the world's major navies. The *Porter* class did see extensive service as ordinary destroyers during the Second World War with only one lost during the conflict.

Armament

The weaponry on the *Porter* class changed dramatically between first entering service in the 1930s and final refits late in the Second World War. When commissioned the *Porters* had eight 5in/38 guns paired in four enclosed mounts with two forward and two aft.

Unlike the 5in/38 dual-purpose gun mounts of the previous *Farragut* class, those on the *Porter* class were only designed for surface fire as a weight-saving measure. All 5in/38 enclosed gun mounts on subsequent US Navy destroyer classes were dual-purpose.

Original anti-aircraft protection depended on two water-cooled quadruple 1.1in (28mm) machine cannons nicknamed 'Chicago pianos' and two .50 calibre (12.7mm) machine guns. Early combat action in the Second World War demonstrated the ineffectiveness of these weapons, as seen in this US Navy report:

Neither the .50 calibre machine gun, effective enough in plane-to-plane fire at point-blank range, nor the 1.1in which the Bureau developed in quadruple mounts in the 1930s, were competent to meet the menace of the Second World War plane. The 1.1in was too heavy to serve as a 'last-ditch' free mount and too light to span the gap between the small machine guns and the 5in guns, even had all its 'bugs' been eliminated. The lack of adequate short-range anti-aircraft guns together with insufficient quantities of the best guns then available created a situation which by 1940 could hardly be termed anything but critical.

The *Porter* class featured the same two stern depth-charge racks as well as the torpedo-launching tube arrangement of the *Farragut* class. However, unlike the *Farragut* class that carried no reload torpedoes, the larger *Porter* class carried eight reload torpedoes. During the Second World War, some of the *Porter* class had K-gun projectors added.

The Aerial Threat

By the late 1930s, as the US Navy became more aware of the severe threat posed by aircraft, the armament array on most of the *Porter* class was significantly upgraded. Increased capabilities came with the replacement of the original four twin 5in/38 gun enclosed mounts, suitable only for surface fire, with four new twin dual-purpose 5in/38 gun enclosed mounts. The new enclosed mount for the twin 5in/38 guns had the designation Mk 32.

From a US Navy manual appears this extract on the ammunition for the new dual-purpose 5in enclosed gun mounts on the *Porter* class:

> Maximum surface range with service rounds having a muzzle velocity of 2,600 feet per second is 18,000 yards [10 miles]. Maximum ceiling is 37,300 feet. The ammunition is two-piece, semi-fixed. The projectile weighs 56.25 pounds, and the powder case (with charge) weighs 28.15 pounds. The projectiles and cases are manually served to the guns from the automatic hoists. The ammunition is of a type that can be fired either electrically (normal method) or by percussion.

Adding to the effectiveness of the dual-purpose 5in/38 guns in anti-aircraft defence was the Variable Time (VT) fuse, first introduced in early 1943. The VT fuse replaced the older-generation time fuses used in 5in projectiles for anti-aircraft use and made the dual-purpose 5in guns as effective as the faster-firing 40mm anti-aircraft guns. A VT-fused projectile was not available for the 40mm anti-aircraft gun until after the Second World War. Due to production limitations some destroyers did not have their intended full complement of 40mm anti-aircraft guns until 1943.

Eventually the quadruple 1.1in (28mm) machine cannons and .50 calibre (12.7mm) machine guns came off the *Porter* class, replaced by 20mm and 40mm anti-aircraft guns. On three of the *Porter* class, late in the Second World War, additional 20mm and 40mm anti-aircraft guns replaced the two centreline quadruple torpedo-launching mounts, the K-guns, and one of the depth-charge racks. Aircraft were then a far greater threat than enemy ships or submarines.

From a wartime US Navy report appears this passage: 'The 40mm developed into the most effective weapon in the fleet. The 20mm, which was the most important weapon during the first two years of the war, was passed by both the 5-inch and 40mm in the percentage of planes knocked down during 1944 and 1945.'

Somers Class

To round out the thirteen examples of the 1,850-ton displacement destroyers allowed by the London Treaty, the US Navy built five examples of what would be labelled the *Somers* class. These were DD-381 and DD-383 through to DD-396. They were completed between 1935 and 1939 and were near-copies of the later-configuration *Porter*-class ships, with four twin dual-purpose 5in enclosed gun mounts and four quad torpedo mounts.

The *Somers* class had an improved but slightly different version of the main propulsion system of the *Benham*-class 1,500-ton destroyers. These included economizers, double-reduction gears and cruising turbines. The *Somers* class had four leading-edge boilers rather than the three in the *Benham* class. Like the *Benham* class, the *Somers* class had only a single stack.

Instead of generating 700° (Fahrenheit) superheated steam as in the boilers of the *Benham* class, the *Somers*-class boilers generated 850° superheated steam. The pressure per square inch (psi) of both the *Benham*- and the *Somers*-class boilers stood at 600psi. This combination of temperature and pressure became standard on all follow-on destroyer classes as well as other US Navy warships.

Like the *Porter* class, the *Somers* class went through a series of extensive armament changes by the end of the Second World War. No two ships of the class were identical in their weapon arrays as they were overhauled at different times. Of the five *Somers*-class destroyers, all but one survived the Second World War. The one lost was not to combat but to a hurricane.

Revised Treaty Destroyers

The second London Naval Treaty, signed by the United States government in 1936, allowed individual destroyer displacement to rise to 3,000 tons and have main guns with a bore size of up to 6.1in. Due to the long lead time required to design and build a new class of 3,000-ton displacement destroyers, the US Navy ordered an upgraded 8ft longer version of the *Benham* class. That decision led to the *Sims* class of twelve destroyers (DD-409 through to DD-420) built between 1937 and 1940, which had a displacement of 1,570 tons.

The *Sims* class was the last to enter service before the official entry of the United States into the Second World War. With the *Sims* class the US Navy reverted to the two-stack arrangement of the *Benham*- and *Somers*-class destroyers, but retained the five single 5in dual-purpose guns in enclosed mounts of the *Benham* class.

Serious Design Issue

Much to the US Navy's dismay, the *Sims*-class vessels showed themselves early on to be dangerously top-heavy in certain conditions, leading to serious stability problems. We see this in an 11 July 1939 US Navy letter: 'But the stability cannot be considered satisfactory when the vessel approaches an assumed extreme light condition which might occur in certain unusual circumstances of peace time or following a prolonged engagement.' The letter stressed that whenever the fuel and reserve feedwater tanks located in a ship's hull fell below 300 tons, the empty tanks had to be ballasted with sea water to maintain ship stability.

As the stability problems would also manifest themselves in follow-on classes based on the *Sims* class, the US Navy ordered extra ballasting as well as topside weight reductions. One of the quad torpedo mounts was removed, as well as one single dual-purpose 5in/38 enclosed gun mount.

Based on the Sims-*Class Destroyers*

There were two very similar but upgraded follow-on destroyer classes to the *Sims*: the thirty examples of the *Benson* and the sixty-six examples of the *Gleaves* with some not completed until 1943. Unlike the *Sims* class, the *Benson* and *Gleaves* classes' DD numbers were not in sequential order. Some older reference sources sub-divide the sixty-six *Gleaves*-class destroyers into the twenty-four ships of the *Livermore* class and forty-two ships of the *Bristol* class.

Like the preceding *Sims* class, the early production examples of the *Benson* class had five single 5in/38 guns in enclosed mounts. To reduce topside weight, later production examples had only four. Rather than the three and later two quad torpedo mounts of the *Sims* class, the *Benson* class was the first to have two quintuple torpedo-launching mounts, a design feature seen on subsequent destroyer classes.

As events transpired, most of the *Benson* class during the Second World War kept only one of their quintuple torpedo-mounts; the other was removed in favour of more anti-aircraft guns. In 1945, thirteen *Benson*-class destroyers had both quintuple torpedo-mounts replaced with even more anti-aircraft guns.

The follow-on *Gleaves* class went through the same armament configuration changes as the *Benson* class. In early 1945, the US Navy ordered that the destroyers of the *Benson* class as well as all the other interwar destroyers remaining in service had their torpedo-launching mounts removed and replaced with more 40mm and 20mm anti-aircraft guns.

As an experiment, in 1943 twelve ships of the *Gleaves* class were fitted with a new British Royal Navy ASW weapon. The weapon fired 7.2in-diameter mortar-type projectiles to a maximum range of approximately 200 yards in front of the ships so fitted; the projectiles were mounted in groups of twenty-four in a fixed mount. The projectiles themselves were referred to as 'Hedgehogs', with the weapon itself labelled the 'Hedgehog'. The heavy recoil produced by the weapon would be a problem and they were ordered removed the following year. The weapon did finally appear on larger post-war US Navy destroyers that were better able to handle the recoil stresses generated.

The *Gleaves* class would be the first destroyer class to have a 'split' propulsion system arrangement in which the ship's four boilers, two per engine, were installed in different compartments separated from each other by intermediate compartments. On previous destroyer classes, the boilers were in a single compartment (referred to as a fire-room) or adjacent compartments (fire-rooms). By separating the

Combat

One of the two *Benson*-class destroyers lost in the Pacific was the USS *Laffey* (DD-459) on the night of 13 November 1942 during the fighting around Guadalcanal. From the US Navy official battle report done the following day appears this passage on a portion of the night battle that caused the sinking of the ship:

> A short time after firing commenced a large unit bore down on the *LAFFEY* from port and only by speeding up was a collision prevented. Torpedoes were fired at this ship, and they were seen to run to the target but did not explode due to the short run and the torpedoes not arming. This large enemy crossed astern of the *LAFFEY* and fire was opened on its bridge superstructure by all guns which would bear. At about this time a large caliber salvo of shells hit the *LAFFEY* in the bridge superstructure and in number two-gun turret, followed very shortly by a torpedo hit at the fantail. Shortly after this, another large caliber salvo hit amidships piercing the after fire-room and electrical workshop. This was the extent of the hits known to have been made on the *LAFFEY* ... By this time it was definitely established that the ship could not be gotten underway and the Commanding Officer gave orders to abandon ship. Abandon ship was conducted in an orderly fashion. Both motor whaleboats and all life rafts except three which caught fire were in the water when a terrific explosion occurred aft. It is believed that the explosion caused the greater percentage of our casualties due to large and small parts of the vessel descending on personnel in the water. Following the explosion, the ship sank immediately.

Some US Navy destroyers played an essential part in the US Army eventually prevailing against strong German opposition on Omaha Beach on 6 June 1944. An extract from a Naval Historical Center publication titled *Destroyers at Normandy: Naval Gunfire Support at Omaha Beach* describes an incident that involved a *Gleaves*-class destroyer, the USS *Doyle* (DD-494):

> I was *Doyle*'s gunnery officer, and recorded one event that took place at 1100: 'Stopped 800 yards off beach Easy Red [the deck log says Fox Red, which I believe is correct]. Observed enemy machine gun emplacement ... Fired two half salvos. Target destroyed. Army troops begin slow advance uphill from beach.' The half salvos were from 5-inch mounts 1 and 2 [*Doyle*'s forward gun mounts], fired almost straight over the bow, one shot at a time. The first anti-aircraft projectile hit the face of the concrete casemate just below the narrow-slit opening and chipped the concrete. The second went straight through the slit and detonated in the German gun room. At the top of the hill was a sandbagged machine gun. It also went quickly.

components of a ship's propulsion plant, the odds of battle damage rendering a vessel powerless were significantly reduced.

Losses

The 108 destroyers of the *Sims*, *Benson* and *Gleaves* classes saw heavy use during the war years. Of the twelve *Sims*-class destroyers lost, five were lost in combat: four in the Pacific to the Japanese and one to the Germans in the Mediterranean. Of the *Gleaves* class, eleven were lost in action: six to the Japanese and five to the Germans. Two others were lost to non-combat causes. Of the *Benson* class three were lost in combat: two in the Pacific and one in the Mediterranean.

The first new class of destroyer authorized after the flush-deckers would be the *Farragut* class of eight ships (DD-348 through to DD-355). Constructed between 1932 and 1935, they initially had no depth-charge racks at the stern, which were added later in 1936. Pictured here are *Farragut*-class destroyers laying a smokescreen during a training exercise. Note the ships have only two stacks instead of the four of the flush-deckers. *(NHC)*

Seen here in dry dock is the USS *Farragut* (DD-348), the lead ship in the *Farragut* class. As propellers turn, they push against the water, with the water pushing back with equal force. The thrust generated by the water pushing back on the propellers is transmitted along a ship's propeller shaft to the shaft's thrust bearing. The thrust bearing allows for the rotation of propeller shafts and transmits thrust to a ship's hull. (*NHC*)

(**Above**) With the *Farragut* class, the US Navy returned to a raised forecastle design as seen in this photograph of the USS *Macdonough* (DD-351). The reason was that the main decks/weather decks of the flush-deckers had taken on too much water in choppy seas, leading to severe corrosion of the ship's exterior equipment such as weapons. *(NHC)*

(**Opposite, above**) Pictured here is the USS *Dewey* (DD-349), a *Farragut*-class destroyer. In the intervening years between the First World War-designed destroyers and the advent of the *Farragut*-class destroyers, both boiler and steam turbine engine technology had significantly advanced. Changes incorporated into the *Farragut*-class design meant destroyers with more durable and reliable propulsion systems. *(NHC)*

(**Opposite, below**) When originally commissioned the *Farragut*-class destroyers had five dual-purpose 5in/38 guns as their main battery, as seen in this example. The pedestal mounts received the designation of the Mk 21. All the destroyer classes after the *Farragut* had power-operated 'base ring stand' mounts with a manual back-up capability. *(NHC)*

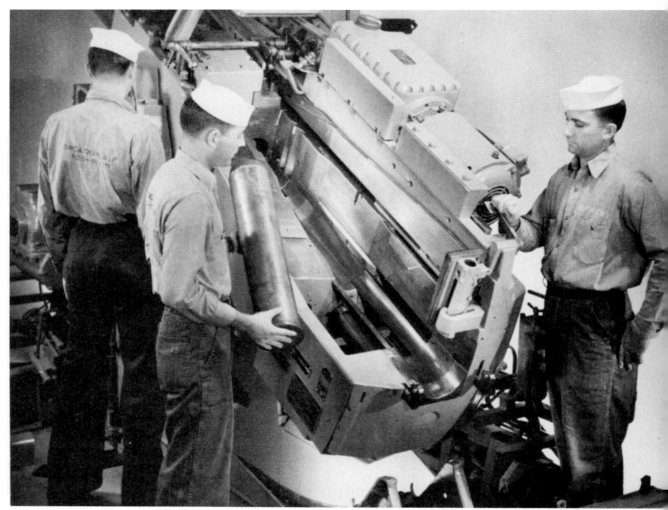

Once the 5in projectile and cartridge case went into a tray seen here located behind the breech of a 5in/38 gun, an electric-hydraulic rammer inserted both into the gun's chamber. The bore was chromium-plated from the forward portion of the powder chamber to the muzzle to prevent corrosion. (*US Navy*)

The *Farragut*-class destroyers were the first to have a 360° traversable gun director for their main battery of 5in/38 guns. The open-topped gun director bore the designation Mk 33, an example of which is pictured here. Located on top of a ship's bridge, it consisted of an electromechanical analogue computer and a sizeable stereoscopic range-finder at the front of the mount as well as a radar antenna. (*NHC*)

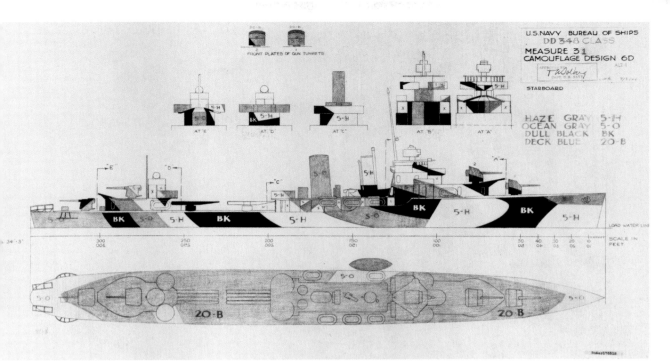

U.S. NAVY BUREAU OF SHIPS
DD 348 CLASS
MEASURE 31
CAMOUFLAGE DESIGN 6D

STARBOARD

HAZE GRAY   5·H
OCEAN GRAY   5·O
DULL BLACK   BK
DECK BLUE   20·B

FRONT PLATES OF GUN TURRETS

The US Navy employed a large number of different camouflage paint schemes during the Second World War for all its warships, including destroyers. In this image we see a camouflage paint scheme for a *Farragut*-class destroyer. Visible is the location of the two quadruple torpedo tube mounts on the vessel's centreline position. That location allowed them to fire over both sides of the destroyer. (*NHC*)

In this Second World War image of the USS *Hull* (DD-350), a *Farragut*-class destroyer, we can see the location of the two quadruple torpedo tube mounts. Some of the new design features of the class and improvements in crew berthing led those serving on older classes of destroyers to refer to the *Farragut*-class destroyers and those that followed by the unofficial nickname of 'gold-platers'. (*NHC*)

U.S.S. DOWNES (D.D. 375)
LEAVING NAVY YARD AFTER COMPLETION
NORFOLK NAVY YARD PORTSMOUTH, VA.
SERIAL NO.147-37 MARCH 1, 1937

(**Opposite, above**) Next in line after the *Farragut*-class destroyers would be eighteen destroyers of the *Mahan* class with the lead ship in the class the USS *Mahan* (DD-364) pictured here. Under the guidance of Rear Admiral Harold Gardner, the US Navy Chief of the Bureau of Engineering, the *Mahan* class had the latest propulsion plant technology based on design work by American and not British firms. (*NHC*)

(**Opposite, below**) In this photograph of the *Mahan*-class destroyer USS *Downes* (DD-375) we can see the three power-operated 5in/38 Mk 24 gun open mounts on the ship's stern. Two were mounted on the stern deckhouse, one at the forward end and one aft. During the Second World War the 5in/38 Mk 24 open gun mount facing forward would be removed and replaced by smaller-calibre anti-aircraft guns. (*NHC*)

(**Above**) In this photograph of the USS *Mahan* (DD-364) we see the two power-operated, base-ring stand-mounted bow 5in/38 guns. Their partial enclosures only provided protection from the elements. These gun mounts received the designation Mk 25. On top of the bridge is an unmanned Mk 33 gun director. The white circles visible in the picture identify recent dockyard alterations and were standard practice in the yards for documentation. (*NHC*)

The last two destroyers of the *Mahan* class (DD-384 and DD-385) had their two forward, power-operated, base-ring stand-mounted 5in/38 guns in enclosed mounts labelled the Mk 30 with an example pictured here. Enclosed mounts provided protection from the weapon's muzzle blast and splinters from incoming fire, but were not referred to as armoured as the US Navy did not consider them 'turrets'. (*Vladimir Yakubov*)

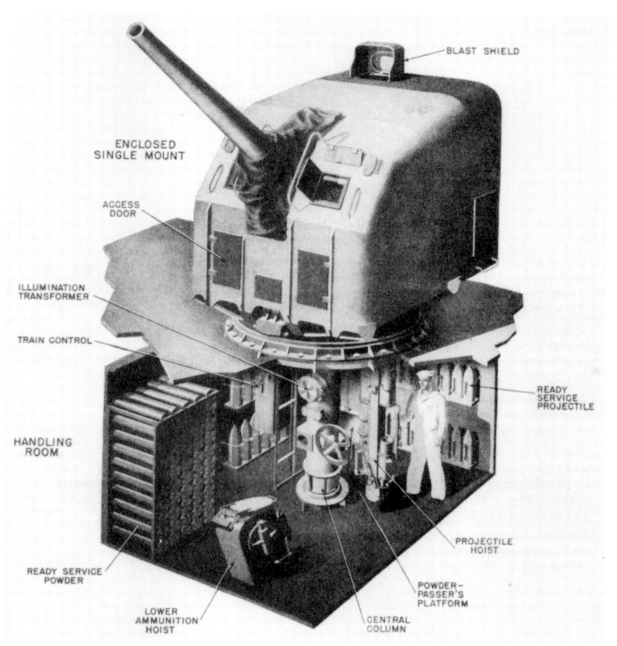

BLAST SHIELD

ENCLOSED
SINGLE MOUNT

ACCESS
DOOR

ILLUMINATION
TRANSFORMER

TRAIN CONTROL

READY
SERVICE
PROJECTILE

HANDLING
ROOM

PROJECTILE
HOIST

READY SERVICE
POWDER

POWDER-
PASSER'S
PLATFORM

LOWER
AMMUNITION
HOIST

CENTRAL
COLUMN

From a US Navy manual is an illustration of a 5in/38 Mk 24 gun mount on a destroyer and its upper handling room located directly below. The latter contained ready rounds, consisting of both projectiles and power (cartridge) cases. The bulk of the gun's ammunition resided in a compartment labelled the lower handling room that transported the projectiles and cartridge cases to the upper handling room by means of power-operated hoists. (NHC)

FORE TRUCK · FOREMAST
YARDARM · YARDARM BLINKER
SPEED CONE · SIGNAL HOIST
FORESTAY · AERIAL
HALYARDS · SPEED CONE
CROW'S NEST · MAIN TRUCK · COMMISSION PENNANT
ANCHOR BALL · MASTHEAD LIGHT · SPEED LIGHT
MAINMAST · PEAK
FLYING BRIDGE · NO.I STACK · GAFF · ENSIGN
NO. 2 STACK
BRIDGE · SPEED FLAG · FLAG STAFF
TORPEDO · FANTAIL
TUBES
NO.2 GUN · PORT SIDELIGHT · STERN
FORECASTLE · BOOT TOPPING
JACK STAFF · STARBOARD SIDE · NO.1 GUN · AFT
HATCH · DAVITS
CHOCK · BITTS · LIFE RAFT
BULL · BOAT BOOM
NOSE
(BOW · LIFE RAFT
CHOCK) · PORT SIDE · FORE AND AFT
STEM · ANCHOR · ATHWARTSHIPS
BOW · FORWARD

(**Opposite, above**) From a wartime US Navy manual is an illustration of a simplified destroyer with many of the external features labelled and various nautical terms applied. The solid part of a ship above the hull is always referred to as the 'superstructure'. The masts, stacks and their related gear emanating from the superstructure are referred to as a vessel's 'top hamper'. (*NHC*)

(**Opposite, below**) Visible in this overhead picture are the torpedo-launching tubes on *Mahan*-class destroyers. This configuration, rather than the two centreline-mounted quadruple torpedo tubes of the preceding *Farragut*-class destroyers, increased the number of torpedoes. US Navy destroyers did not carry reload torpedoes as did the destroyers of the Japanese Navy. (*NHC*)

(**Above**) For the control of a destroyer's torpedo tube launching mounts, there was the manned Mk 27 director, pictured here. A fire-control instrument, it computed and transmitted an electrical signal of the torpedo's intended course order and gyro angle to the torpedo course indicators located at the manned torpedo tube launching mounts. A firing key at the director, when closed, completed the firing circuit which launched the torpedo/torpedoes. (*NHC*)

(**Opposite, above**) The Projector Mk 6 or 'K-gun' (shown here) addressed problems presented by the First World War-era 'Y-gun'. The latter had to be centreline-mounted to throw depth-charges off both sides simultaneously, and required clear fields of fire to clear the sides. K-guns could be mounted closer to the rails, leaving the valuable centreline space for other uses. (*NHC*)

(**Above**) American President Franklin D. Roosevelt and the US Congress enacted many military construction programmes during the 1930s, including the construction of twenty-two new destroyers based on the last two ships of the *Mahan* class. These comprised the very similar ships of the *Gridley* (four), *Bagley* (eight) and *Benham* classes (ten). Pictured here are two *Gridley*-class destroyers with their now-enclosed Mk 33 gun directors.

(**Opposite, below**) The USS *Stack* (DD-406), a *Benham*-class destroyer, is shown here during the Second World War. The *Benham* class and the preceding *Gridley* and *Bagley* classes had two major design features not seen on any other destroyer class before or during the Second World War. These were a single exhaust stack, and a total of four quadruple torpedo launching tubes, two on either side of the ships' main deck. The latter reflected increased awareness of the striking power of torpedoes. (*NHC*)

(**Opposite, above**) During the interwar period, and like other navies, the US Navy failed to appreciate the ever-growing threat of aerial attack. Pictured here on a ground mount is an example of the Browning Machine Gun, Cal. .50, M2, Water-Cooled, Flexible, a type of light anti-aircraft gun installed on the destroyers of the time. Results from US Navy testing against aircraft in 1929 proved very disappointing. (*National Archives*)

(**Above**) The much-awaited replacement for the water-cooled, .50 calibre M2 machine gun on US Navy warships took place in 1935, with the introduction of the Quadruple 1.1in Machine Cannon pictured here. Originally there was no gun director for the weapon. Rushed into production, its complexity resulted in an inferior reliability and it quickly fell out of favour with the US Navy. (*Vladimir Yakubov*)

(**Opposite, below**) Nicknamed the 'Chicago Piano', the Quadruple 1.1in Machine Cannon mount weighed in between 10,500lb and 14,000lb. The original gun mounts were not power-operated, only manually trained and elevated. Later model mounts were power-operated and controlled by a gun director. Elevation went up to 111° with a maximum depression of minus 15°. (*NHC*)

(**Above**) In the light anti-aircraft weapon category, the US Navy placed two guns into service as the replacement for the water-cooled, .50 calibre (12.7mm) machine gun and the Quadruple 1.1in (28mm) Machine Cannon. One of these, the pedestal-mounted, 20mm Single Mount Mk 4 is pictured here. It was approved for service by the US Navy in November 1940. (*National Archives*)

(**Opposite, above**) In 1942, the US Navy considered the pedestal-mounted 20mm (Oerlikon) Single Mount Mk 4 pictured here a very effective anti-aircraft weapon, accounting for up to 48.3 per cent of enemy aircraft. By 1944, this figure had dropped to just 25 per cent as engagement ranges increased and the Japanese switched to night attacks during which only radar-guided weapons were effective. (*Vladimir Yakubov*)

(**Opposite, below**) From a US Navy manual is an illustration of the pedestal-mounted 20mm Single Mount Mk 4. By 1945, the limited usefulness of the weapon led the captain of one US Navy destroyer to suggest in a report: '... heavy continuous fire as the ship's best defense and recommended replacing 20mm with 40mm [anti-aircraft guns] ... the 20mm had a negative psychological value, the saying among the crews being "when the 20mm opens fire, it's time to hit the deck."' (*US Navy*)

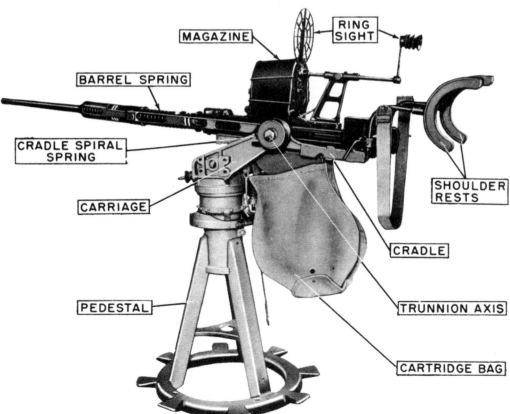

The replacement for the Quadruple 1.1in Machine Cannon in the US Navy proved to be the water-cooled 40mm gun in twin mounts labelled Mk 1. Each barrel could fire a high-explosive projectile weighing almost 2lb at up to 160 rounds per minute. Besides the standard high-explosive round, there were armour-piercing and incendiary rounds provided for the weapon. (*Vladimir Yakubov*)

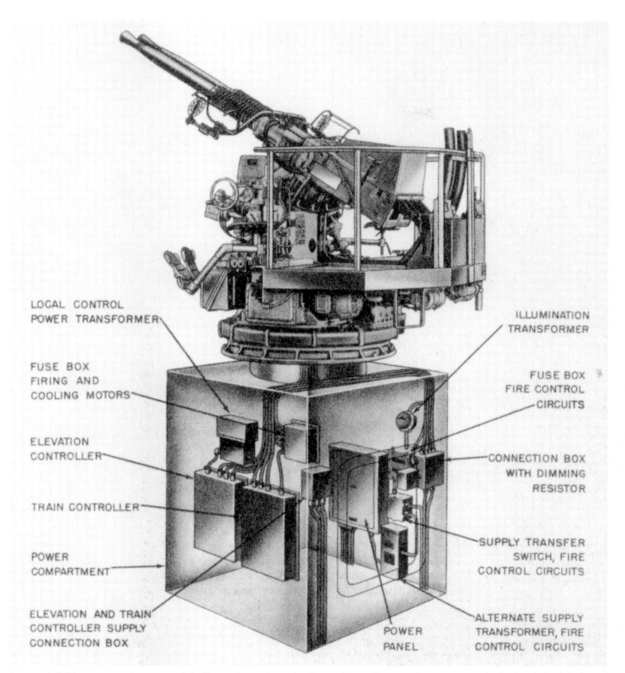

LOCAL CONTROL
POWER TRANSFORMER

ILLUMINATION
TRANSFORMER

FUSE BOX
FIRING AND
COOLING MOTORS

FUSE BOX
FIRE CONTROL
CIRCUITS

ELEVATION
CONTROLLER

CONNECTION BOX
WITH DIMMING
RESISTOR

TRAIN CONTROLLER

SUPPLY TRANSFER
SWITCH, FIRE
CONTROL CIRCUITS

POWER
COMPARTMENT

ELEVATION AND TRAIN
CONTROLLER SUPPLY
CONNECTION BOX

POWER
PANEL

ALTERNATE SUPPLY
TRANSFORMER, FIRE
CONTROL CIRCUITS

From a US Navy manual appears this illustration of a twin 40mm base-ring stand gun mount designated the Mk 1 and the compartment below it that housed the electrical power system for the weapon. With the electrical power system, the weapon could be remotely-controlled by a gun director. If the gun director or power went down, the gun crew could aim and train the weapon manually. (*US Navy*)

(**Above**) The 40mm guns of the Twin Mount Mk 1 seen here could be elevated to an angle of approximately 90° from their horizontal position, or depressed 15° below the zero position. The mount's power system had a maximum train speed of around 50° per second in automatic control. (*US Navy*)

(**Opposite, above**) Although the interwar-designed destroyer classes' anti-aircraft defences were updated for service in the Second World War, they were unable to handle the topside weight of the 40mm twin gun mounts Mk 1. This led to thirteen interwar-designed destroyers being armed with the US Army's M1 single-gun version of the 40mm gun, an example of which is pictured here. (*National Archives*)

(**Opposite, below**) In the 1930s, the US Navy decided it needed larger destroyers as command and control ships for smaller destroyer classes. These received the label of 'destroyer leaders' with thirteen built in two different classes: eight *Porters* (DD-356 through to DD-363), with an example pictured here; and five *Somers* (DD-381, 383, 394, 395 and 396). Despite their new title, they retained the prefix 'DD'. (*NHC*)

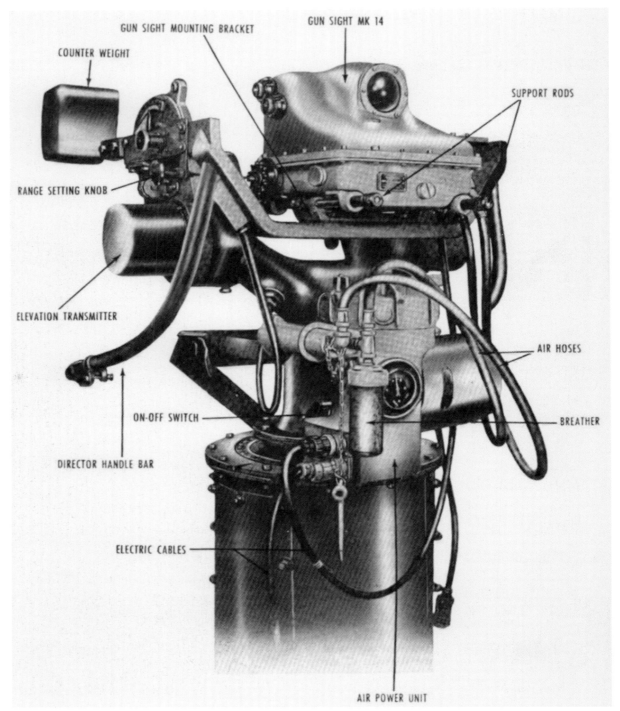

COUNTER WEIGHT

GUN SIGHT MOUNTING BRACKET

GUN SIGHT MK 14

SUPPORT RODS

RANGE SETTING KNOB

ELEVATION TRANSMITTER

AIR HOSES

ON-OFF SWITCH

BREATHER

DIRECTOR HANDLE BAR

ELECTRIC CABLES

AIR POWER UNIT

Before 1940, the US Navy showed little interest in gun directors for its light anti-aircraft guns, figuring that open sights and tracer fire would suffice. By 1940, it became clear to the US Navy that the aerial threat was much more serious than originally believed. The result would be the 1940 development of the Director Mk 51 pictured here. By the war's end, 15,000 units of the Mk 51 came off the production lines. (*US Navy*)

The US Navy originally armed the *Porter*- and *Somers*-class destroyer leaders with eight power-operated 5in/38 guns paired in four twin Mk 22 single-purpose mounts. Pictured here are two of the base-ring stand Mk 22 single-purpose (surface fire only) enclosed mounts on a *Porter*-class destroyer leader. During the war years, the single-purpose 5in gun mounts were removed and replaced by base-ring stand, power-operated, dual-purpose 5in/38 gun mounts. (*NHC*)

(**Above**) Torpedoman First Class Fred Parmentier at his station on the USS *Jouett* (DD-396), a *Somers*-class destroyer leader. He is awaiting orders to release depth-charges during operations in the South Atlantic in May 1942. Release controls for the stern depth-charges are on the ship's bridge. Note the signal lamp, the telescope, the 'talker' headset he is wearing, and the torpedo director on his left. (*NHC*)

(**Opposite, above**) The last of the interwar-designed US Navy destroyers built before America's official entry into the Second World War would be the twelve ships of the *Sims* class (DD-409 through to DD-420) with the lead ship in the class, the USS *Sims* (DD-409), shown here. They originally had five power-operated, dual-purpose base-ring stand 5in/38 gun mounts. That number dropped to just four mounts in wartime to reduce topside weight. (*NHC*)

(**Opposite, below**) The USS *Leary* (DD-158), a *Wickes*-class First World War era-designed destroyer, was the first US Navy warship fitted with radar, as seen here in April 1937. At the time it was a temporary arrangement. The radar set's antenna is attached to the barrel of the 4in/50 pedestal-mounted deck gun in the background of the photograph. (*NHC*)

The *Sims*-class destroyers were the first to have the Mk 37 'gunfire control system' fitted (pictured here). It would be the replacement for the earlier Mk 33 gun-director on destroyers. Unlike the Mk 33 that started its service career without radar and associated antenna, the Mk 37 had a radar set and associated antenna. (*NHC*)

(**Opposite, above**) A ghosted view of the crew positions in a Mk 37 gun fire-control system. It would first be tested in 1939 and quickly became standard equipment on all the destroyer classes following the *Sims* class. The stereo-scopic range-finder and radar/s employed with the Mk 37 established the line of sight to a target as well as the range. In the anti-aircraft role, it determined relative target bearing and elevation. (*NHC*)

(**Opposite, below**) A key component of both the Mk 33 and Mk 3 gun directors was their stereoscopic range-finders. The range-finder itself was a 15ft-long metal tube with an eyepiece at the centre and windows (sights) at either end. Inside the tube were lens and prisms, as well as precision mechanisms for moving them. When the person manning the range-finder looked through the eyepiece, he would see the target and range marks. (*US Navy*)

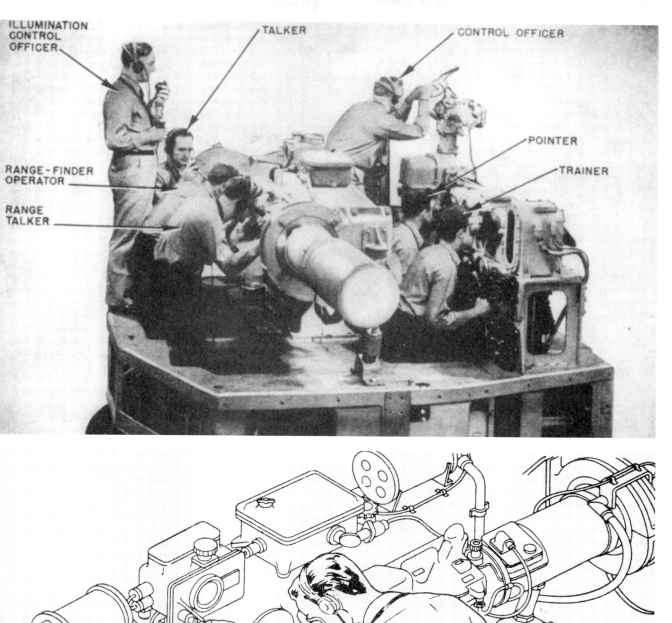

ILLUMINATION CONTROL OFFICER

TALKER

CONTROL OFFICER

POINTER

TRAINER

RANGE-FINDER OPERATOR

RANGE TALKER

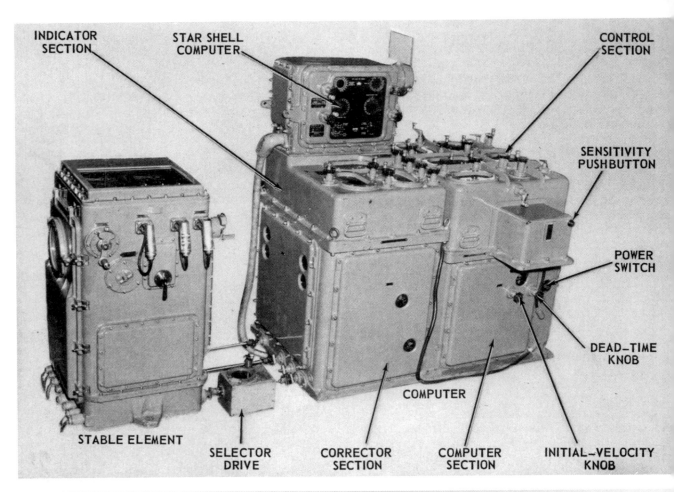

INDICATOR SECTION

STAR SHELL COMPUTER

CONTROL SECTION

SENSITIVITY PUSHBUTTON

POWER SWITCH

DEAD—TIME KNOB

STABLE ELEMENT

SELECTOR DRIVE

CORRECTOR SECTION

COMPUTER

COMPUTER SECTION

INITIAL—VELOCITY KNOB

10

417

(**Opposite, above**) The electromechanical (analogue) computer (often referred to at the time as a 'range keeper') for the Mk 37 gunfire control system had the designation Computer Mk I and is pictured here. From the information supplied to it during the target acquisition process, it computed the needed corrections, applied them to the uncorrected target elevation and bearings coming from the director, and sent the corrected gun elevation and bearing orders to the powered gun mounts. (*US Navy*)

(**Above**) On entering US Navy service, the *Sims*-class destroyers had the same torpedo-launching mount arrangement as the *Mahan*-class destroyers, with one quadruple torpedo-launching mount on the ship's centreline affixed on a pedestal and a quadruple torpedo tube on either side of the vessel's main deck. Later that was changed to two centreline quadruple torpedo-launching tubes, shown here in a wartime image. (*NHC*)

(**Opposite, below**) On 6 April 1945 a kamikaze struck the USS *Morris* (DD-417), a *Sims*-class destroyer, just below the main deck near the foremost 5in/38 Mk 30 enclosed mount. The picture shows the ship after most of the debris had been cleared away. Patched up, the ship returned to the San Francisco Naval Shipyard (later renamed Hunter Point) for repairs on 18 June 1945. However, it would be deemed not worth repairing and was pulled from service by the end of the year. (*NHC*)

(**Above**) Between 1938 and 1943 a total of thirty examples of the *Benson*-class destroyers were built with the USS *Hilary P. Jones* (DD-427) seen here prepared for launching. They were an improved version of the previous *Sims*-class destroyers. A new design feature for the class was an arrangement of alternating boiler- and engine-rooms to improve their survivability when struck by torpedoes. It was a design feature found on all subsequent US Navy destroyer classes. (*NHC*)

(**Opposite, above**) With the introduction of alternating boiler- and engine-rooms on the *Benson*-class destroyers, the design reverted to the two-stack configuration seen here with the USS *Frazier* (DD-607). During the Second World War, the *Frazier* sank one or perhaps two Japanese submarines with depth-charges. With the help of another destroyer, the *Frazier* forced another Japanese submarine to the surface, ramming the enemy submarine and sending it to the bottom. (*NHC*)

(**Opposite, below**) On 30 December 1944, a kamikaze struck the USS *Gansevoort* (DD-608), a *Benson*-class destroyer, and caused extensive damage. Several fires started, and thirty-four crew were killed or wounded. Despite the damage suffered, the ship did not sink and was towed to a nearby anchorage for temporary repairs. (*NHC*)

ABT 50°

N° 2 STACK FORCED FOR'D &
TO PORT BY EXPLOSION

STB'D. 20 M/M GUN FOUNDATION

WALKWAY

UPTAKE MATERIAL

PORT LIFE
NET BURNED
COMPLETELY

BULWARK

RUPTURE IN SHELL PLT'G
BY PLANE & BLOWN OUT
BY EXPLOSION

ABT 12-0"

ABT 4'-0" ENTIRE "G" STRAKE
& 3/4 OF "F" STRAKE

3434-45

DD-608

② CLOSE-UP OF PORT SIDE IN DAMAGED
AREA

SHIP'S PHOTO   7 JAN. 1945

(**Opposite**) Two *Gleaves*-class destroyers prepared for launching. After launching, they will move to a fitting-out pier, and shipyard workers will install the missing 5in/38 Mk 30 gun mounts and the Mk 37 gunfire control system. The *Gleaves*-class ships were near-identical to the *Benson* class and built concurrently, with American shipyards building a total of sixty-six examples between 1938 and 1943. (*NHC*)

(**Above**) Shown here in March 1945 is the USS *Ludlow* (DD-438), a *Gleaves*-class destroyer. Commissioned in March 1941, the ship saw heavy action in the November 1942 invasion of North Africa, the July 1943 invasion of Sicily and the Anzio landing in January 1944. With the end of the war in Europe in May 1945, the ship sailed to the Pacific but arrived too late to see combat in that area of operation. (*NHC*)

The *Benson*- and *Gleaves*-class destroyers were the first US Navy destroyers to be armed with two centreline quintuple torpedo-launching tubes, like the example pictured here. The typical destroyer torpedo by the Second World War was the 3,841lb Mk 15 that had an 825lb high-explosive warhead. Note the large searchlights in the background on either side of one of the ship's two stacks. (*NHC*)

The *Gleaves*-class destroyer USS *Kearny* (DD-432) took a German torpedo on 16 October 1941. The damage appears in this photograph of the ship, as she waits for temporary repairs in an Iceland bay. The fact that the ship did not sink would be attributed to her alternating boiler- and engine-room design that prevented the vessel losing power from all her engines. (*NHC*)

An example of artwork by McClelland Barclay in which the US Navy gun crew of a 4in/50 gun on a pedestal mount is in action. Barclay was an accomplished painter, illustrator, sculptor and jewellery designer by the time he became a lieutenant in the US Naval Reserve in 1938. His wartime artwork was often intended for use in US Navy recruitment posters. (NHC)

In this painting by McClelland Barclay, a US Navy sailor is preparing to load a depth-charge onto a depth-charge projector known as the K-gun. In the background, a depth-charge is in the air after launching. Barclay died on 18 July 1943 when a Japanese submarine's torpedo sank the ship on which he was stationed, LST-342. (NHC)

An artist's impression of the USS Navy *Fletcher*-class destroyer the *Charles Ausburne* (DD-570), engaged in combat with Japanese surface ships. During her time in service, from 1943 to the end of the war, the *Charles Ausburne* accounted for a wide range of different types of enemy vessels that earned her eleven battle stars. *(NHC)*

Seen here on a US Navy destroyer during the Second World War is the four-man crew of the twin-barrel 20mm anti-aircraft gun in the background. Both single and double-barrel configurations were known as the 'Oerlikon', named for the Swiss firm that had developed them. The sailors shown are a far cry from the muscular square-jawed sailors portrayed in McClelland Barclay's artwork. *(NHC)*

The USS *Hopewell* (DD-681), seen here in the 1960s, was a *Fletcher*-class destroyer commissioned in September 1943. In this picture the ship appears very much in her Second World War configuration. She saw combat in both the Korean and Vietnam Wars. The US Navy decommissioned the *Hopewell* in January 1970; she was later sunk as a target in February 1972. (*US Navy*)

Pictured in 1965 is the USS *Rowan* (DD-782), a *Gearing*-class destroyer, commissioned in March 1945. She arrived too late to see combat during the Second World War. She saw action during the Korean War and was struck on a couple of different occasions by North Korean coastal defence guns. She went through the FRAM I programme in 1963, with this photograph reflecting the configuration changes. (*US Navy*)

The USS *Gyatt* (DD-712), a *Gearing*-class destroyer, was commissioned in July 1945, too late to see combat in the Second World War. She was named for Marine Private Edward Earl Gyatt, posthumously awarded the Silver Star for gallantry during the taking of the island of Tulagi in the Guadalcanal campaign. In 1957, the ship became the first US Navy destroyer armed with a surface-to-air missile (SAM) known as the Terrier. Reflecting her new role, she became the DDG-712 and later the DDG-1 as seen in this photograph. (*NHC*)

Commissioned in May 1960 was the USS *Preble* (DDG-46), a *Farragut*-class destroyer. During the Vietnam War, she suffered some minor damage inflicted by North Vietnam artillery. Originally armed with the Terrier surface-to-air missile, she eventually had the much more capable 'Standard' SAM installed. Decommissioned in November 1991, the ship went on for scrapping in 2003. (*NHC*)

Passing through the Suez Canal is the USS *Tattnal* (DDG-19), a *Charles F. Adams*-class destroyer commissioned in April 1963. Originally armed with the Tartar surface-to-air missile, she would later be upgraded with the Standard SAM that has a secondary role as an anti-ship missile. The *Tattnal* would be decommissioned in January 1991 and finally scrapped in March 2000. (*NHC*)

Heading to the bottom is the USS *Tower* (DDG-9), a *Charles T. Adams*-class destroyer commissioned in June 1961. The ship saw a great deal of service during the Vietnam War in the shore bombardment role and in the rescue of many downed pilots and air crew. The ship would be decommissioned in October 1990 and sunk as a target as pictured in October 2002. (*NHC*)

In a dead calm sea state is a *Spruance*-class destroyer, one of thirty-one constructed for the US Navy between 1972 and 1983. When first envisioned, they were to be primarily ASW platforms. Later they had anti-ship weapons and land-attack missiles such as the Tomahawk fitted. The last ship in the class went through its decommissioning in 2005. (*US Navy*)

Inside a *Spruance*-class destroyer, a sailor maintains watch over a damage-control diagram of the entire ship during a training exercise. The *Spruance* class was the replacement for the large inventory of Second World War-designed destroyer classes that, despite upgrades, in many cases had reached the end of their service lives. (*US Navy*)

A sailor is placing a 70lb 5in projectile into a storage rack on board a *Spruance*-class destroyer. The ships had two 5in/54 Mk 42 gun mounts, one forward and one aft. These guns were primarily intended for shore bombardment but retained some limited effectiveness as anti-ship and anti-aircraft weapons. (*US Navy*)

Pictured here is an *Arleigh Burke*-class destroyer, the US Navy's replacement for the *Spruance*-class destroyers. Unlike its predecessors that had an all-aluminium superstructure, the *Arleigh Burke* class's superstructure is constructed of steel as it offers a higher degree of survivability despite higher weight. The US Navy would commission the first ship in the class in July 1991. (*US Navy*)

Taken inside an *Arleigh Burke*-class destroyer is this image of a portion of the vessel's darkened Combat Information Centre (CIC). The electronic heart of the ships' CICs is the AEGIS Combat System, the system that can detect and track more than 100 potential targets at a time. In its newest configuration, it can detect and track intercontinental ballistic missiles (ICBMs). *(US Navy)*

The planned replacement for the *Arleigh Burke*-class destroyers was to be thirty-two units of the *Zumwalt* class; the lead vessel in the class is pictured here. Unfortunately, serious design issues and continuing cost overruns resulted in only three ships in the class entering service. Part of the problem was the US Navy pushing ahead with technology that had not yet matured and hence was lacking reliability. *(US Navy)*

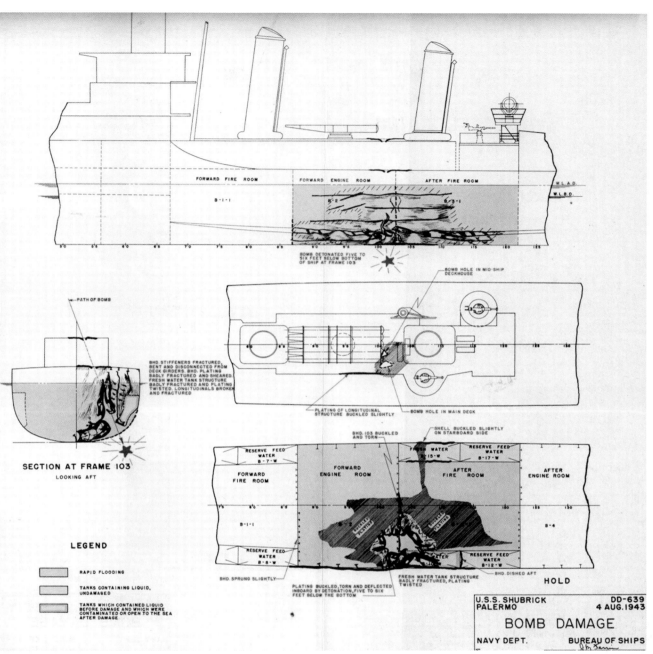

On the night of 4 August 1943, while in support of the Allied invasion of Sicily, the USS *Shubrick* (DD-639), a *Gleaves*-class destroyer, had an enemy 500lb aircraft bomb penetrate her main deck and explode within the hull, killing nine men with another twenty wounded. Shown in this official US Navy line illustration is the damage incurred by the ship. (*NHC*)

Chapter Three

Second World War Destroyers

On 11 June 1940, Congress authorized funding for the first twenty-five examples of a new class of destroyers initially assigned the designation of the '445 class' and eventually labelled the '*Fletchers*'. Conceived in October 1939, they descended from the previous *Benson*- and *Gleaves*-class destroyers.

As there would be a two-year time lag before the first batch of *Fletcher*-class destroyers could be commissioned, Congress went on to authorize the funding necessary for the building of additional destroyers from the preceding *Greaves* class. The US Navy design bureaus thought this was a wise decision at that time but had advised Congress the month before that 'immediate and urgent need' existed 'for destroyers of increased ruggedness and seaworthiness, armament, speed and protection as embodied in the design of 445 class.'

Due to continued battlefield success by the German military, especially the fall of France on 16 June 1940, the American Congress passed the 'Two-Ocean Navy Act' on 19 July 1940. It provided funding for the US Navy to increase its strength by some 70 per cent, which translated into 257 warships, with 115 to be destroyers.

Into Service

The first of the commissioned *Fletchers* would be the USS *Nicholas* (DD-449) on 6 June 1942, just two days after the American victory at the Battle of Midway. The last of the 175 *Fletcher*-class destroyers was commissioned on 22 February 1945.

As more capable *Fletcher*-class destroyers entered service, the interwar-class-designed destroyers were assigned to secondary roles, such as convoy escort or shore bombardment where their deficiencies in anti-aircraft weaponry, compared to the *Fletchers*, proved less critical.

Bigger and Better

The *Fletchers* were the first class of US Navy destroyers not bound by any interwar treaty restrictions. Thus their initial standard displacement was 2,050 tons, making them the largest US Navy destroyer class yet built. The late-war addition of ever more anti-aircraft weaponry (40mm and 20mm) raised the class's displacement to approximately 2,900 tons.

Part of the reason for the *Fletchers*' increase in size was driven by the US Navy's requirement for a destroyer with sufficient endurance for vast distances of the Pacific Ocean. The ships needed to carry much more fuel. In addition to the possibility of combat with the forces of Nazi Germany, the US Navy had long anticipated and planned for a possible war with Japan. On paper, the *Fletchers* had a maximum range of approximately 5,500 miles when cruising at 15 knots.

Into Combat

Nineteen *Fletchers* were sunk in combat, with another six so severely damaged that they were considered to be not worth rebuilding. Of the more than 58,000 sailors who served on the 175 *Fletchers* during the Second World War, about 2,200 died, with approximately 2,600 wounded. Some *Fletchers* lost more than half their crews in action.

An illustration of the combat damage endured by a *Fletcher*-class destroyer appears in the following passage about damage to the USS *Albert W. Grant* (DD-649) in a post-war US Navy report. During an engagement on the evening of 25 October 1944, the ship would be straddled by friendly gunfire:

> Projectiles riddled the ship fore-and-aft. Fragments of a hit on 40mm mount No. 1 detonated some 40mm ready service ammunition and started a fire. Repeated hits on the topside damaged the boats, galley, radio room, forward stack, and uptakes. ... Power to the armament was completely interrupted. The battery remained operable manually except 5-inch gun No. 5 and 40mm mount No. 4, both of which were immobilized by fragments. Electric power was lost forward, and all lighting except emergency circuits went out. All communications, including radio and radar, were reported inoperable.

The *Albert W. Grant* survived her terrible mauling and went off to a shipyard for repair. Re-entering service on 11 March 1945, she saw out the remainder of the war without any further damage. In July 1946, she had her one and only decommissioning.

General Description

The *Fletchers* were flush-decked rather than having the raised forecastle of the interwar-designed destroyer classes. Crew complement could be anywhere from 240 men up to approximately 300. The extra manpower came about due to the addition of ever more anti-aircraft guns and added equipment that had to be manned, such as sonar and multiple radars.

Fitted with the same propulsion plant as the *Gleaves* class, the early-production *Fletchers* had on paper a maximum speed of 37 knots. That speed dropped as *Fletchers*' displacement grew during the war years. Another contributing factor would have been normal wear and tear on the ships' propulsion plants.

With a length of approximately 377ft, the *Fletchers* were 28ft 0.5in longer than the *Benson* and *Gleaves* classes. With a beam of almost 40ft, they were about 4ft wider than their predecessors. The increase in the *Fletchers'* length and beam significantly improved handling and stability in rough sea conditions in spite of light conditions (being low on fuel and reserve water).

The *Fletchers'* improved stability allowed the class to comfortably handle the topside weight of five dual-purpose 5in single enclosed gun mounts, a design short-coming of the previous *Sims*-, *Benson*- and *Greaves*-class destroyers that had to have one of their 5in single enclosed gun mounts removed due to stability issues.

Torpedo Damage

The design of the *Fletcher* class's components delivered excellent stability, allowing for limited armour plating not seen on previous US Navy destroyer classes around certain key areas. Unfortunately, the lack of any armour protection around the *Fletcher*-class hulls made them very vulnerable to mine and torpedo damage.

On 30 January 1943, the USS *La Vallette* (DD-448), a *Fletcher*-class destroyer, was struck by a torpedo delivered by a Japanese aircraft. In the after-action report is this passage on what then occurred:

> Although the vessel was turning to port at the time to avoid being hit, one torpedo dropped by a burning plane 300 yards distant, struck the port side in way of the forward engine room at frame 94, about 8½ feet below the water-line. A 40-foot column of water deluged the vessel. LA VALLETTE was shaken violently from stem to stern and seemed to lift bodily out of the water. The forward engine room and fire-room flooded immediately. The after fire-room started to flood gradually. There was no apparent list. Both engines stopped and all power was lost temporarily. No fires resulted.

Such was the impact when *La Vallette* was hit that the two quintuple torpedo-launching mounts were damaged, as seen in this extract from the after-action report:

> The detonation broke the tension links for all ten torpedoes. The torpedoes in the forward mount slid out of the tubes, hit the bulwark on the main deck and then fell into the sea. The torpedoes were running when they left the tubes, and the propellers of some were seen turning over when the torpedoes cleared the side. The torpedoes in the after mount slid forward about three feet and also were running in the tubes. These were fired immediately before any further shock or motion of the ship could cause them to slide clear of the tubes. The loss of the ten torpedoes acted as a jettisoning measure to somewhat improve the stability characteristics.

Despite the damage to *La Vallette* the ship remained afloat, was towed away to a repair site and eventually returned to duty. However, on 14 February 1945 she struck a Japanese mine and once again suffered damage. As before, the ship did not sink and would eventually be repaired at a shipyard. She once more returned to duty to see out the rest of the Second World War. Her one and only decommissioning took place in 1946.

Mine Damage

On 18 August 1943, the USS *Abner Read* (DD-526), a *Fletcher*-class destroyer, struck a Japanese mine. From a US Navy study of mine damage is this passage describing what caused a 75ft long and 18ft wide section of the ship's stern to break off from the remainder of the hull and sink:

> Apparently, the detonation lifted the stern and caused a tension crack in the bottom plating and compression buckles in the upper portion of the shell plating and main deck at frame 170. The stresses at this point may have been augmented by the flexural vibration which occurred as the result of the detonation. Flooding of ruptured compartments aft added sufficient weight to the stern to cause rupture of the remaining effective plating and longitudinals at frame 170. The stern then drifted aft, sliding off the starboard shaft, and sank. The failure at frame 170 does not denote a structural deficiency in the longitudinal strength of the 445-class destroyer. This type of failure will in all probability occur only when a mine or torpedo detonates under the stern in a location close to that of *Abner Read*.

Abner Read was towed to a shipyard and underwent major repairs, including the addition of a new stern. The destroyer returned to duty on 6 December 1943. On 1 November 1944, a Japanese suicide plane managed to drop a bomb down one of the ship's stacks before crashing into the ship herself. A massive internal explosion rocked the vessel before she sank. All but twenty-two of her crew were saved by nearby US Navy ships.

Surface-Search Radar

The *Fletchers* were the first US Navy destroyers to have a surface-search radar (designated as the SG) as standard equipment when commissioned. The SG's ability to detect large targets ranged from 30,000 to 60,000 yards. Its antenna was mounted on the ship's foremast just below the air-search radar antenna.

According to a US Navy manual:

> Surface search radars measure the range and bearing of surface contacts to assist in navigating the ship, or to send surface target information to the weapon direction system [gun directors]. They are also effective in detecting low flying aircraft since their radar energy is concentrated at low angles of elevation.

With the surface-search radar came a Plan Position Indicator (PPI) radar display that presented a map-like overview of the area covered by the radar allowing for target engagement without actual observation of the target or targets. The PPI was located in the main superstructure of *Fletcher*-class destroyers. The many advantages of radar on warships appear in an extract from a US Navy wartime manual on the subject:

> Radar, generally speaking, can reach out beyond the visual horizon. It can detect through darkness, fog, and smoke as well as through sunshine. You no longer have to wait until the enemy appears over the horizon before you know several facts about him – his presence, number, size, course, and speed. You can be preparing a plan of action before the enemy even knows where you are. Thus, radar enables your ship to 'shoot the guns', even in the dark [blind-firing], and to make hits with the first or second salvo.

Before radar, all US Navy destroyer classes depended on the use of searchlights during the hours of darkness. However, there were serious drawbacks: the lights revealed a ship's location, were quickly destroyed by enemy gunfire, and were limited to a maximum range of 4,000 yards under optimal conditions. As a back-up to their radar, the *Fletcher*-class destroyers were equipped with searchlights during the Second World War.

Surface-Search Radar Examples

On the night of 7 April 1943, the surface-search radar of a *Fletcher*-class destroyer, USS *Strong* (DD-467), detected something that was quickly identified as a Japanese submarine just rising from the depths. From the official US Navy report of the engagement appears this extract on what happened next: 'Commenced firing immediately 5-inch, 20 and 40mm when a large size submarine fully surfaced appeared in the center of a searchlight beam. Range about 700 yards. The 5-inch began to hit immediately, the 20mm and 40mm sprayed the decks and hull from bow to stern.'

As the Japanese submarine quickly began to sink stern-first, the *Strong* headed towards its location. Once it arrived, the destroyer's crew noticed a strong smell of diesel oil. The *Strong* then proceeded to drop a total of sixteen depth-charges during two runs over the submarine's last location before being ordered to rejoin the task force to which she belonged.

Following a night surface engagement that occurred on 2 November 1943 between the US Navy and the Japanese Navy, the senior officers of the USS *Spence* (DD-512), a *Fletcher*-class destroyer, wrote this passage:

> It has been conclusively demonstrated that destroyer gunnery when carried out properly, results in early and continued hitting. The enemy has not yet mastered radar for search and gunnery. It was specifically noted that they fired at our gun flashes, except for the period in which we were hit. Their gunfire was slow,

disorganized and inaccurate. The value of the 2,100-ton class destroyers [*Fletchers*] has certainly asserted itself as an effective fighting ship.

Air-Search Radar

Located on top of the *Fletcher* class's foremast (just above the surface-search radar) was an air-search radar antenna. The radar set itself, depending on the model, received the prefix designation SA, SC or, later in the war, SR, followed by a model number. The air-search radar's job was to fix a target's position in two coordinates: range and bearing. There was no height-finding radar initially fitted on the *Fletchers*.

The primary function of air-search radars was to warn a ship of the presence of aircraft at extreme range, although the radars could also be used to detect surface targets if required. To determine if an approaching plane was friendly or hostile, the air-search radar had an interrogator device that sent out a coded signal. The aircraft's transponder, if so equipped, sent back an encrypted message to confirm its identity. If not, the plane was considered hostile. That information was then transmitted to the fire-control radar.

From a US Navy report titled 'Anti-aircraft Summary' dated April 1945 comes this extract on the various methods that Japanese suicide planes tried to avoid shipborne air-search radar during 1944 and 1945:

> The approach of suicide planes is characterized by tactics designed to take advantage of the weaknesses of our search radar equipment. These tactics are in general as follows: flying at altitudes exceeding 20,000 feet to make best use of radar null areas, or flying very low over water to avoid early detection. Making a series of dives and climbs, rarely flying a straight course when within 40 miles of the target ships ... Trailing in the shadow of the IFF of friendly planes returning to their bases ... Approaching in small groups from different bearings and at different altitudes to increase the radar interception problem.

Fire-Control Radar

The initial fire-control radar antenna on the *Fletcher*-class destroyers (on the roof of the ship's main gun director, the Mk 37) received the designation Mk 4. A much more capable version that consisted of two separate radar antennas joined together began appearing on the *Fletcher*-class destroyers in 1944 and was assigned the designation Mk 12/22. The job of the Mk 12/22 was target acquisition and tracking for the ship's 5in main gun battery in both ship and aircraft engagements.

In the anti-aircraft role the Mk 4 and the Mk 12/22 radar had a more complicated task than when employed in the surface fire-control role. This was for greater target speeds, the need for target elevation measurements and the requirement for auto-mated radar tracking.

Anti-Aircraft Fire-Control Systems

There were two general types of anti-aircraft fire-control systems employed on US Navy destroyers during the Second World War. The first was the 'linear-rate system' which determines changes in target position, course and speed by measuring the distance between successive target positions. The second was the 'relative-rate system' which measures the angular velocity of the line of sight to determine target motion.

The linear-rate system was the primary means for control of 5in dual-purpose guns for both surface and aerial fire. The relative-rate system of fire-control developed during the Second World War when increased aircraft speeds made it necessary to reduce the time required to generate an anti-aircraft fire-control solution since the allowable time was limited by the relatively short range of 20mm anti-aircraft guns. Eventually, the relative-rate system was designed for destroyers to control both 40mm anti-aircraft guns as well as the 5in/38 dual-purpose guns.

Relative-rate anti-aircraft fire-control systems determine changes in target position by measuring the angular velocity of the line of sight. From a US Navy manual:

> If you keep a finger pointed at an airplane, the rate at which your arm and finger must move to follow the flight of the plane is a rough measure of the angular velocity of the line of sight. Relative-rate systems measure this angular velocity and correct for the time of flight and curvature of trajectory.

Very effective at longer ranges and somewhat effective at intermediate ranges, the Mk 37 proved less successful at tracking and engaging suicide aircraft at shorter ranges. One reason for this was the weight and size of the Mk 37. It was unable to traverse quickly enough to shift from one fast-moving short-range target to another.

A passage from a US Navy report dated 8 October 1945 mentioned one method to resolve the Mk 37's inability to deal with fast-moving short-range aircraft: 'Many ships placed 5-inch batteries under the control of manually operated auxiliary directors [Mk 51 or Mk 49] as a method of engaging enemy planes with gunfire under surprise conditions. In the event the target was picked up at long range, control was shifted to the main director.'

One US Navy wartime report suggested that by tweaking the Mk 37 and having a well-trained crew, some of the difficulties that the 5in gun had in engaging fast-moving, short-range enemy aircraft could be overcome.

Enemy Countermeasures

Japanese pilots employed other methods to confuse warships' air-search and fire-control radars. On 3 April 1945, the fire-control radar team on USS *Bush* (DD-529), a *Fletcher*-class destroyer, identified the enemy's use of 'window', also known as 'chaff'. Made from aluminium foil strips cut to resonate at a particular radar frequency, the descending cloud of chaff effectively jammed targeting radars:

> On the evening of 3 April at about 2200 a group of enemy planes closed and dropped window around the ship at a range of ten to thirteen miles, completely blocking the SC-2 screen. The window appeared on the Mk-4 screen and only by judicious tracking was gun control able to distinguish between true and false targets. The window dissipated in about 20–30 minutes. This indicates that the Japanese are becoming more proficient with the use of window or that our [radar] operators need more training. Japanese knowledge of our radar frequency set-up is increasing.

At the very end of the war in the Pacific, a few of the *Fletcher*-class destroyers had radar countermeasure (RCM) equipment installed. The reason for this appears in a passage from a wartime US Navy manual:

> The enemy has two purposes in using [electronic] radar countermeasures: first, he hopes to prevent us from obtaining any accurate or useful information about his forces by the use of our radars; and second, he wishes to get information about our forces by listening to our radars. The radar countermeasures methods that may be used in accomplishing these purposes are of four types: interception, jamming, deception, and evasion.

Torpedo Armament

As first appeared on the *Benson* class and later the *Gleaves* class, the *Fletchers* featured two quintuple torpedo-launching mounts installed on the ships' centreline. The 21in-diameter torpedoes fired from the quintuple torpedo-launching mounts were labelled the Mk 15. The Mk 15 entered US Navy service in 1938 and was the replacement on destroyers for the earlier Mk 11 and 12 torpedoes.

Weighing in at 3,841lb, the Mk 15 torpedoes were 24ft in length, had an 825lb warhead and were powered by a steam turbine engine. Their maximum firing range was 15,000 yards at a speed of 26.5 knots. They could also be set to travel at two other speeds. However, the faster the speed setting, the shorter the range. The Mk 15 was the last anti-ship torpedo placed into service by the US Navy.

The torpedo-launching mounts had two directors designated the Mk 27 to aid in acquiring and engaging targets. They were on either side of the ship's pilot house. The crew of a torpedo-firing mount was informed of the desired course by a torpedo course indicator fitted to their mount. Receiving firing data from the Mk 27 directors, the torpedo-firing mount crew manually trained their mount to match the information presented on their indicator. The personnel manning the director fired the torpedo or torpedoes.

Sonar

In the early 1930s, a small number of interwar *Wickes*- and *Clemson*-class destroyers had the first shipboard sonar system, designated the QA, fitted to the bottom of their hulls. However, the sonar system's transducers had no covering, so the flow noise generated by the ship's movement greatly reduced the sonar's effectiveness. Transducers turn electrical energy into sound waves, which when reflected by a submerged submarine's hull helped to locate them.

By the time the *Fletcher* class appeared, the ships had transducer (sonar) domes for the QCJ and QCL series sonar systems under the fixed keel. Later in the war, they were fitted with retractable transducer (sonar) domes for the improved QGB or QJB series sonars.

From a post-war US Navy manual appears a passage describing the sonar employed for most of the Second World War:

> The principal sonars in use … projected a narrow beam of sound into the water, and target indications were returned as audio responses from a speaker or headset. A thorough search was a slow process in which the operator hand-trained the transducer in increments of 2½ degrees to 5 degrees, according to search doctrine in force.

A post-war 1945 US Navy report commented that the searchlight-type sonar could not track late-war very fast German submarines, or submarines fitted with effective sonar countermeasures. If a destroyer exceeded 15 knots the ship's own noise would mask the echoes returned from submerged submarines. With a wartime range of only 1,500 to 2,000 yards, the US Navy decided that in the future its sonar sets had to have a minimum range of 5,000 yards.

By the closing stages of the Second World War, the US Navy had perfected a new type of search sonar referred to as 'scanning or azimuth search sonar' and designated the QJB. An omnidirectional sonar, it sent out sound waves (pulses) in all directions simultaneously. It then scanned or sampled all the returning echoes received and generated a video image for the human operator. At the same time, it also reviewed the returning echoes' characteristics to aid in determining the range to a potential submarine by means of a range recorder.

ASW Weapons

Both the interwar and *Fletcher*-class destroyers had a limited array of ASW weapons to engage and destroy submerged submarines. The oldest was the depth-charge, invented by the British Royal Navy during the First World War, and stored typically in two pairs of structural metal racks on the ship's fantail, dating back to the US Navy flivvers.

At the beginning of the Second World War, the US Navy employed two different-sized depth-charges: the First World War Mk 6 containing 300lb of TNT, and the interwar Mk 7 containing 600lb of TNT. The former originally had a maximum depth of 300ft that would be increased to 600ft by the middle of 1942. The Mk 7's maximum depth remained at 300ft throughout the war.

The Mk 6 and Mk 7 depth-charges were drum-shaped, hence their popular nick-name of 'ash cans'. Their shape slowed their descent underwater, allowing the target more time to evade them. By 1943, a new 600lb depth-charge designated the Mk 9 entered US Navy service with a maximum depth of 600ft. Its teardrop shape allowed it to sink faster, and had vanes to hold a pattern during descent so it could reach the intended targets before the target moved too far from the last known location.

Due to the weight of the Mk 7 and Mk 9 they were restricted to the two stern racks of *Fletcher*-class destroyers, with each rack containing eight depth-charges. The 300lb Mk 6 was fired from K-gun projectors, with up to six on late-war *Fletchers*. The ships themselves had onboard storage for additional depth-charges.

The US Navy conducted experimental work on a 520lb depth-charge designated the Mk 8. It had a proximity fuse that could be set off with a magnetic or acoustic fuse. The results were not positive, and the US Navy dropped the programme.

Fletcher-*Class Derivatives*

Even before the first of the *Fletcher*-class destroyers entered service, the US Navy began thinking about a replacement class. Several designs were considered. However, in the end, it was decided to expedite delivery. A slightly redesigned version of the *Fletcher* class, the *Allen M. Sumner* class, was placed into production.

Some 15in wider and 15in deeper in draft than the *Fletcher* class, the *Sumner* class had two rudders (instead of the single rudder of its predecessor) to increase man-oeuvrability. Manoeuvrability is an important feature when engaged in ASW. Class displacement on paper rose to 2,220 tons, although as with the *Fletchers*, wartime changes and additions would eventually push up class displacement. Like the *Fletcher* class, the *Sumner* class had one of its two quintuple torpedo-launching mounts removed for additional anti-aircraft guns.

Initially, the US Navy had anticipated planning for seventy examples of the *Sumner* class, but in the end, only fifty-eight came out of the shipyards with the rest cancelled due to the conclusion of the Second World War. The first, commissioned on 26 January 1944, was the lead ship in the class, the *Allen M. Sumner* (DD-692). The last ship of the class, commissioned in October 1946, was the USS *Henley* (DD-762). Twelve of the *Sumner*-class destroyers were converted into fast mine-layers.

Of the *Sumner*-class ships that served in the Second World War, four sank and two others were so severely damaged that rebuilding them was not an option after the war. Six shipyards switched over from production of the *Fletcher* class to build ships of the *Sumner* class.

Main Gun Armament

The primary external design feature that identifies a *Sumner*-class destroyer would be the replacement of the five single 5in/38 enclosed gun mounts of the *Fletcher* class with three twin 5in/38 enclosed gun mounts. Two were located forward and one aft. A partial description of the new twin 5in/38 enclosed gun mounts and how they worked on the *Sumner*-class destroyers appears in this extract from a wartime US Navy manual:

> The guns can be loaded at any point between the maximum and the minimum angles of elevation. They are served and loaded separately. Gun elevation and mount train are performed, in normal operations, by high-speed electric-hydraulic power drives that can be controlled either automatically by a remote [gun] director [the Mk 37] or locally from the mount handwheel station.

The twin 5in/38 enclosed gun mounts on the *Sumner* received the designation Mk 38. Although in theory the enclosed gun mounts could be manually trained if the power went down, the accepted reality was that it could not take place quickly enough to engage fast-moving aerial targets, especially at shorter ranges.

The projectiles and propellant cartridge cases that made up the 5in rounds were brought up from the magazines in the ship's hull by vertically-orientated powered hoists. Both the projectiles and propellant cartridge cases were loaded separately by hand into a tray behind the gun breech and then pushed into the breech by a power-operated rammer.

Anti-Aircraft Action

Reflecting the ever-growing threat from aircraft, the *Sumner*-class destroyers went to sea with even more 20mm and 40mm anti-aircraft guns than the ships of the pre-ceding *Fletcher* class. As built, they originally had two quadruple 40mm gun mounts and four twin-mount 40mm anti-aircraft guns fitted, in addition to eleven 20mm anti-aircraft guns. The effectiveness of the anti-aircraft weaponry on the *Sumners* became apparent during the first half of 1945.

Between March and May 1945, the US Navy deployed a number of destroyers of the *Fletcher* and *Sumner* classes off the coast of Japan. Their job was to identify incoming flights of enemy suicide planes heading towards the US Navy's invasion fleet operating off Okinawa. Labelled 'radar picket ships', they were provided with a height-finding radar (nicknamed 'pencil beam radar') and extra radio equipment. The additional radios were employed to control and direct combat air patrol (CAP) assets. The CAPs were intended to intercept enemy aircraft before they could reach the fleet.

In many cases, the Japanese suicide pilots decided that rather than continue to Okinawa they would attempt to sink the radar picket ships. From a July 1945 US Navy report appears this extract describing what a single *Sumner*-class destroyer, the *Hadley* (DD-774), did to defend herself on the morning of 11 May 1945:

> For 20 minutes the *Hadley* fought off the enemy single-handed, being separated from the *Evans* [another *Sumner*-class destroyer], which was out of action, by 3 miles and from the four small support ships by 2 miles. Finally, at 0920, ten enemy planes which had surrounded the *Hadley*, four on the starboard bow under fire by the main battery and machine guns [20mm and 40mm], four on the port bow under fire by the forward machine guns, and two astern under fire by the after-machine guns, attacked the ship simultaneously. All ten planes were destroyed in a remarkable fight, and each plane was definitely accounted for. As a result of this attack, the *Hadley* was (1) hit by a bomb aft (2) by a BAKA bomb [rocket-powered aircraft] seen to be released from a low-flying Betty [twin-engine bomber] (3) was struck by a suicide plane aft (4) hit by a suicide plane in rigging.

Gearing-Class Destroyers

Ordered soon after the *Sumners* was the *Gearing* class. The US Navy originally planned for 152 examples, but in the end only 98 were built, with the rest cancelled due to the end of the Second World War. A lengthened version of the previous class, the *Gearing*-class destroyers were approximately 14ft longer with about the same beam, allowing for the inclusion of larger fuel tanks.

Displacement grew to 2,616 tons. Crew complement came in at approximately 350 men. Only four of the ninety-eight *Gearing*-class destroyers were commissioned before the official end of the Second World War. These included DD-710, the lead ship of the class, the USS *Gearing*, and three others, the last of which was commissioned before the end of the war on 3 May 1945. The final *Gearing*-class destroyer would be commissioned in 1952.

Unofficial Labels

The longer length of the *Gearing* class resulted in the unofficial label of the 'long-hulled' destroyers and the *Sumner* class became the 'short-hulled' destroyers. Both were typically referred to as 2,200-ton destroyers, even though the *Gearing* class had an official standard displacement of 2,400 tons.

The *Fletcher* class was unofficially referred to as the 'DD-445 class' based on the hull number of the lead ship in its class. That same unofficial labelling system would be applied to the *Sumner*- and *Gearing*-class destroyers; hence they respectively became the 'DD-692 class' and the 'DD-710 class'.

Combat Information Center

The *Sumner-* and the *Gearing*-class destroyers were the first to feature a built-in command and control centre in their superstructure referred to as the 'Combat Information Center' (CIC). These were later retrofitted to the *Fletcher*-class destroyers and interwar-designed destroyer classes. In a US Navy document titled *Handbook for Destroyers: Pacific Fleet*, dated 24 June 1943, appears the following passage:

> The development of the Combat Information Center as an integral unit of the ship's organization is possibly one of the most drastic and rapid changes in our shipboard experience. Apparently, the need for such an agency, a tactical plot or a ship's operation officer, existed before the war without our general realization of that fact. When radar was developed, it simply furnished us with more information than we were able to handle in any way other than with this tactical plotting and evaluating agency.

From a wartime US Navy manual is this description of a CIC: '... is a space containing radar equipment, plotting devices and communications (internal and external) equipment manned by specifically trained personnel and charged with keeping the commanding officer and higher commands embarked informed of the location, identity, and movement of friendly and/or enemy aircraft and surface ships within the area.'

The various electronic devices present (including a Plan Position Indicator (PPI) scope) in a US Navy destroyer's CIC provided the watch officer with a much clearer picture of what was going on outside the vessel (especially during the hours of darkness) than that available to the captain (or command duty officer (CDO) in charge on the ship's bridge when the captain was not present). Eventually, some ships' captains preferred commanding their vessel from its CIC rather than from their bridge.

From a US Navy report written about an early August 1943 engagement between US Navy destroyers and Japanese destroyers that resulted in the sinking of three out of four of the latter: 'This action proved the value of an efficient CIC in destroyers. What might otherwise have been a confusing series of reports and orders became a coordinated flow of evaluated information because of CIC.'

(**Opposite, above**) The largest class of destroyer ever built for the US Navy proved to be the *Fletcher* class, with an example pictured here during trials (USS *Nicholas* (DD-449), one of the most-decorated Second World War destroyers). A total of 175 came out of American shipyards between March 1941 and February 1945. Bigger and better than the interwar-designed destroyers, they proved extremely capable vessels with both the range and firepower necessary to successfully perform a wide variety of roles. *(NHC)*

(**Opposite, below**) Due to the size and increased displacement of the *Fletcher*-class destroyers, they went to sea with an impressive array of weaponry. Weapons included five of the dual-purpose, power-operated, single 5in/38 Mk 30 mounts as seen in this photograph, and two centreline quintuple torpedo tubes. At the fantail of the *Fletchers* were two racks for storing a total of twenty-eight depth-charges. *(NHC)*

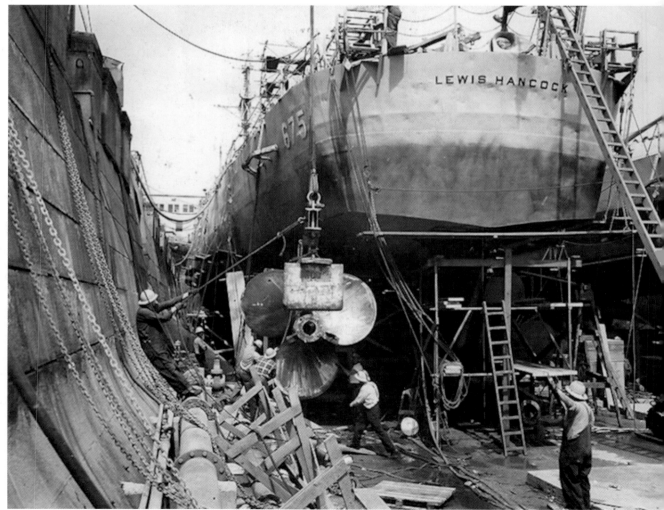

(**Opposite, above**) With an originally listed displacement of 2,100 tons, the *Fletcher*-class destroyers when fully loaded quickly rose in weight to a displacement of almost 2,900 tons. The lowest number in the class was the lead ship, the USS *Fletcher* (DD-445), although it proved to be the USS *Pringle* (DD-477) that the US Navy commissioned first. The last *Fletcher*-class destroyer commissioned in February 1945 would be the USS *Rooks* (DD-804). (*NHC*)

(**Opposite, below**) A new propeller goes onto a *Fletcher*-class destroyer. As with the interwar-designed destroyer classes that preceded it, the *Fletchers* had only a single rudder. Eleven shipyards took part in the construction of the *Fletcher* class, with the Bath Iron Works building the largest number at thirty-one. On average it took eleven months from the day a ship's keel was laid down to the ship's commissioning. (*NHC*)

(**Above**) One of the two engine-room control boards on a *Fletcher*-class destroyer. Like the last of the interwar-designed destroyer classes, the *Gleaves*, the *Fletcher* class had an alternating boiler (fire-room) and engine-room arrangement. To enhance the survivability of the two pairs of adjoining fire-rooms and engine-rooms they were separated by watertight bulkheads that rose to the ships' main deck. (*NHC*)

USS HATFIELD (DD-231)

```
USS HATFIELD (DD-231)
Length:          314 feet
Displacement:    1,215 tons
Complement:      6 officers, 95 enlisted
Armament:        Five-inch guns (4); 21-inch torpedoes
                 (12) in four triple mounts
```

USS MAHAN (DD-364)

```
USS MAHAN (DD-364)
Length:          341 feet
Displacement:    1,500 tons
Complement:      8 officers, 150 enlisted
Armament:        Five-inch, 38 cal. dual-purpose guns (5);
                 21 inch torpedoes (12)
```

USS FLETCHER (DD-445)

```
USS FLETCHER (DD-445)
Length:          376 feet
Displacement:    2,100 tons
Complement:      9 officers, 264 enlisted
Armament:        Five 5"/38 dual-purpose guns in five mounts;
                 Two mounts of five 21 inch torpedoes.
```

In this image, we see the dramatic increase in size and operational parameters between an example of a First World War-designed destroyer class, an interwar-designed destroyer class, and finally, the Second World War-designed *Fletcher* class. The last, like the previous interwar-designed destroyer classes, went through extensive modification during the war in both armament and electronics. (*NHC*)

U.S.S. O'BANNON - D
June 21, 1942 - INCLINING

In this shipyard image, we see the two centreline quintuple torpedo tubes of a *Fletcher*-class destroyer. Late in the Second World War as the threat from Japanese warships dramatically decreased and the threat from Japanese aircraft became much more serious, the aft quintuple torpedo tube was removed and replaced by more 40mm anti-aircraft guns. (*NHC*)

Due to muzzle blast from the 5in/38 gun mount pictured here, the aft quintuple torpedo tube had a small circular blast enclosure to shield the three human operators. The forward quintuple mount, which lacked that feature, received the designation Mk 14. The aft quintuple mount, having the enclosure, bore the designation Mk 15. (*NHC*)

(**Above**) The job of cleaning and corrosion prevention is never-ending, as typified by these sailors tasked with maintaining a quintuple torpedo tube. The 21in Mk 15 torpedoes launched with a black-powder impulse. The torpedo itself fell under the heading of an air-stream type with the first 4ft containing the warhead. (*NHC*)

(**Opposite, above**) Looking forward from the fantail of a *Fletcher*-class destroyer, we see three armour-shielded, pedestal-mounted 20mm Single Mount Mk 4s. The weapon's circular magazine contained anywhere between 60 and 100 20mm rounds. In theory, the weapon had a rate of fire of 450 rounds per minute. The weapon's crew could replace the barrel in as little as thirty seconds. (*NHC*)

(**Opposite, below**) As the late-war kamikaze threat continued to take its toll on US Navy warships, it became clear that the projectiles fired by the pedestal-mounted 20mm Single Mount Mk 4 lacked the stopping power required to destroy or deflect incoming aircraft. To improve the weapon's performance, work began in early 1944 on the twin-mount configuration seen here and labelled the Mk 24, with the first production examples appearing in late 1944. (*Vladimir Yakubov*)

For the latter part of the Second World War in the Pacific Ocean theatre of operation, the 40mm guns in the twin mount Mk1 (as pictured here) and the quadruple mount Mk2 became the most successful anti-aircraft weapon system for defending the destroyer classes that mounted them. The rounds fed into the automatic loaders of individual guns came in clips of four, inserted by the gun crew. (*NHC*)

Initially, the early-production *Fletcher*-class destroyers depended on the Quadruple 1.1in (28mm) Machine Cannons. By June 1943, they were authorized ten of the 40mm twin mounts Mk 1. Circled here is a 40mm twin mount that replaced a 20mm single-mount gun in front of this *Fletcher*-class destroyer's superstructure. Circled above the ship's bridge is a Mk 51 gun director. *(NHC)*

MK 51 DIRECTOR (WITH MK 14 SIGHT)

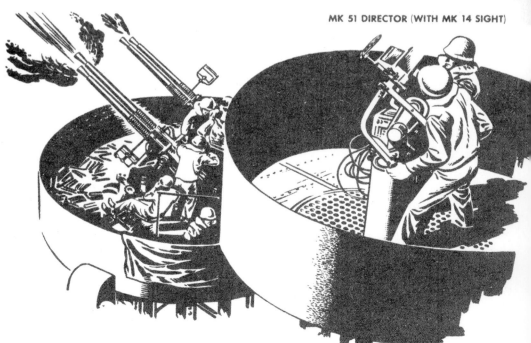

TRANSMITTER
RECEIVER

ANTENNA
HOUSING

OPTICS

RADAR

CONFIDENTIAL
U.S.S. BB 62
MARK 49 DIRECTOR WITH
MARK 19 RADAR,
LOOKING FWD.
PHILA. NAVY YARD   OCT. 29,1943.

(**Opposite, above**) By 1944, some of the *Fletcher*-class destroyers had their anti-aircraft defence upgraded with the 40mm quad mount Mk 2 pictured here. They weighed approximately 30,000lb with a thin armoured shield fitted. By the end of the war with Japan, the US Navy would be looking for a more potent and longer-ranged anti-aircraft gun than the 40mm. (*Paul and Loren Hannah*)

(**Opposite, below**) For the best line of sight, the Mk 51 gun director seen here in this illustration from a US Navy manual (controlling a quadruple 40mm gun mount Mk 2) was mounted as high on a ship as possible. The Mk 51 was developed in secret by Dr Charles Draper of MIT (Massachusetts Institute of Technology) and assigned to the Sperry Gyroscope Company for production. (*US Navy*)

(**Above**) As a possible replacement for the open Mk 51 gun director, the US Navy installed on some warships, including *Fletcher*-class destroyers, the enclosed Mk 49 as pictured here. Whereas the Mk 51 depended on a human operator for elevation and training, the Mk 49 was power-operated. It also had an attached radar antenna. Unfortunately the Mk 49 proved unreliable in service and production was terminated by the US Navy in mid-1943. (*NHC*)

CONTROL
TALKER

DIRECTOR
POINTER

CONTROL
OFFICER

DIRECTOR
OPERATOR

WIND BOX
OPERATOR

RADAR
OPERATOR

The late-war replacement for the Mk 51 gun director was the radar-equipped Mk 52 gun director seen here in a US Navy manual illustration with its crew. It had been originally designed to operate only with 3in and 5in guns in the anti-aircraft role; however, those in combat wanted it dedicated as a gun director for the 40mm guns. The last-minute change meant that only 200 had entered service by the end of the Second World War. (*US Navy*)

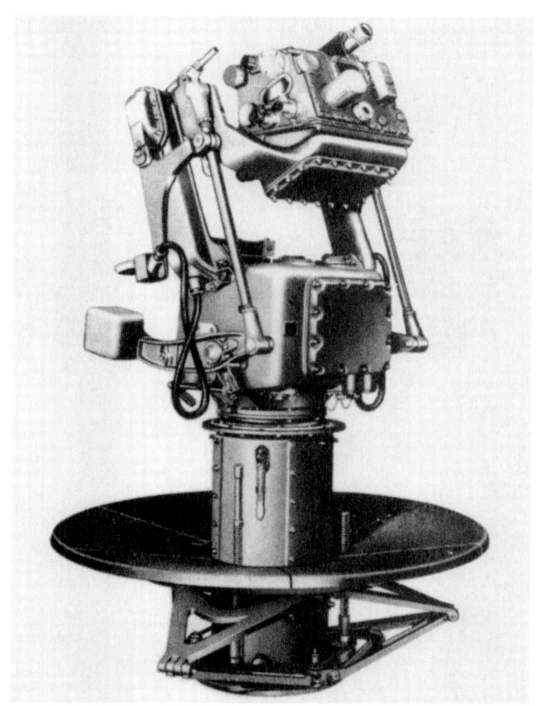

A dedicated 40mm gun director developed during the Second World War was the Mk 63 pictured here that had its associated radar antenna affixed to the 40mm gun mounts it controlled. The radar operator was located in a compartment directly below the director. Manually-operated, the direction operator relied on a telescope for acquiring targets. (US Navy)

A major external design difference between the 175 *Fletcher*-class destroyers built during the Second World War was the design of their respective bridges. Early-production examples had rounded streamlined bridges copied from previous interwar-designed destroyer classes including the *Sims*, *Benson* and *Gleaves* classes. (*NHC*)

Royal Navy experience in the early stages of the Second World War had shown that streamlined bridges were a problem. As the officers on a ship's bridge tried to maintain visual observation of aerial threats, they had to pass through their ship's intervening pilot house which separated their two open flying bridges. The solution adopted by the Royal Navy and seen here on a *Fletcher*-class destroyer would be a square bridge design. (NHC)

The large Mk 4 radar antenna on the early examples of the Mk 37 director fitted to *Fletcher*-class destroyers and interwar-designed destroyer classes during the Second World War had some design shortcomings. To correct those issues the Mk 4 radar antenna seen here mounted on the roof of a Mk 37 director had a second smaller Mk 22 height-finding radar antenna fitted to one side nicknamed the 'Orange Peel'. (NHC)

RADAR ANTENNA

OBSERVATION HATCH
(closed)

SLEWING SIGHT

TELESCOPE PORTS

RANGEFINDER

RANGEFINDER

BARBETTE

(**Above**) Beginning in 1948, the Mk 37 director had its Mk 4 and Mk 22 radar antenna combination replaced by a much smaller and lighter dish radar antenna seen here in this picture from a US Navy manual. It received the designation of the Mk 25 and combined both tracking- and height-finding features of the former Mk 4/Mk 22 combination. (*US Navy*)

(**Opposite**) The rectangular radar antenna at the very top of the ship's foremast is an 'SC' long-range air-search radar. It could detect a bomber at a range of 92 miles and a fighter plane at 46 miles. The circled curved antenna below it is an 'SG' surface-search radar. The circled vertical antenna is a 'BL' radar beacon for an Identification-friend-or-foe (IFF) system. (*NHC*)

Two US Navy sailors are shown here monitoring a sonar stack in a Second World War destroyer. Sonar would first appear as a viable method of detecting submarines in the closing stages of the First World War. Invented by the allies, it consisted of directional hydrophones (microphones) attached to the bottom of a ship. American scientists applied the name 'SONAR', an acronym for 'Sound Navigation and Ranging'. *(NHC)*

In this line illustration from a US Navy manual are the various elements that combine to allow warships to detect submerged submarines. It involves bouncing an audible signal against a submarine hull and measuring the time between signal generation and the return signal echo. The sonar equipment can then measure the range and determine the submarine's bearing. (NHC)

Seen here on a *Fletcher*-class destroyer's forward hull is the location of the fixed sonar dome that protected the directional hydrophones (referred to as transducers) located within. The sound waves generated by the transducers travelled through the water at 4,700 to 5,300ft per second. Later-model sonar domes on US Navy destroyers would be retractable. (NHC)

(**Above**) In this photograph, a sailor is preparing a depth-charge for firing from a Mk 6 depth-charge projector, better known as the 'K-gun'. *Fletcher*-class destroyers had six projectors, with three on either side of their main deck. The K-gun's range was adjustable, based on the charge amount, to anywhere between 60 and 150 yards. (*NHC*)

(**Opposite, above**) The two inclined depth-charge racks seen here in May 1944 on the stern of a *Fletcher*-class destroyer, the USS *Killen* (DD-593), contain the teardrop-shaped Mk 9 depth-charge. It would be the wartime replacement for the long line of ashcan-shaped depth-charges employed by the US Navy. The Mk 9 had a 200lb high-explosive warhead; the later-production examples could reach a depth of 1,000ft. (*NHC*)

(**Opposite, below**) In this picture taken in 1962, a decommissioned *Fletcher*-class destroyer has just been struck by a US Navy torpedo during a firing trial. Reflecting the lack of armour, they were sometimes referred to as 'tin cans'. The emphasis on speed in destroyer designs led to the popular nickname of 'Greyhounds of the Sea'. (*US Navy*)

(**Opposite, above**) On 6 April 1945, the *Fletcher*-class destroyer the USS *Leutze* (DD-481) had pulled alongside the stricken USS *Newcomb* (DD-586), another *Fletcher*-class destroyer that had been struck by three kamikazes. When another kamikaze struck the *Newcomb*, it slid across the ship's main deck to explode against the fantail of the *Leutze*. By successfully controlling flooding, the crew of the *Leutze* saved the ship. (*NHC*)

(**Above**) Anchored off Omaha Beach at Normandy on the night of 12 June 1944, *Gleaves*-class destroyer USS *Nelson* (DD-623) was torpedoed by a German E-boat. The torpedo struck the ship's stern, blowing it off as clearly seen in this photograph. Despite the damage, which cost four killed and nine wounded, the ship remained afloat. Towed to Boston Naval Shipyard in Massachusetts, she was returned to service after extensive repairs. (*NHC*)

(**Opposite, below**) On 10 June 1945, a kamikaze crashed near the *William D. Porter* (DD-579), a *Fletcher*-class destroyer. As its debris passed underneath the ship, a bomb from the plane detonated, rupturing the ship's hull and starting fires. Despite the crew's best efforts, the ship eventually went down, though miraculously no crewman was killed or seriously injured. In this picture, two US Navy amphibious landing ships are taking off the crew as they abandon ship. (*NHC*)

Pictured on an *Allen M. Sumner*-class destroyer is one of its three twin 5in/38 twin enclosed gun mounts, labelled the Mk 52. The external bracing shown in the photograph also appeared on the enclosed gun mount's sides. The bracing typically only appeared on the most forward twin 5in gun mount of *Sumner*-class destroyers, as its exposed location suffered the most from rough seas. *(NHC)*

(**Opposite, above**) In a pristine camouflage paint scheme is the USS *Charles S. Sperry* (DD-697), one of fifty-eight examples of the *Allen M. Sumner*-class destroyers built during the Second World War. An improved version of *Fletcher*-class destroyers, it retained the same length as its predecessors but was 15in wider and 15in deeper in draft. *Sperry* would be transferred to the Chilean Navy in 1974, serving until 1990. *(NHC)*

(**Opposite, below**) The increased beam, depth and displacement of *Allen M. Sumner*-class destroyers allowed for more topside weight on the ships. The US Navy took advantage of this feature by replacing the five power-operated 5in/38 single gun mounts of previous *Fletcher*-class destroyers with three power-operated twin 5in/38 gun mounts labelled the Mk 38. Two of the latter appear on the USS *Lofberg* (DD-759), commissioned in April 1945. *(NHC)*

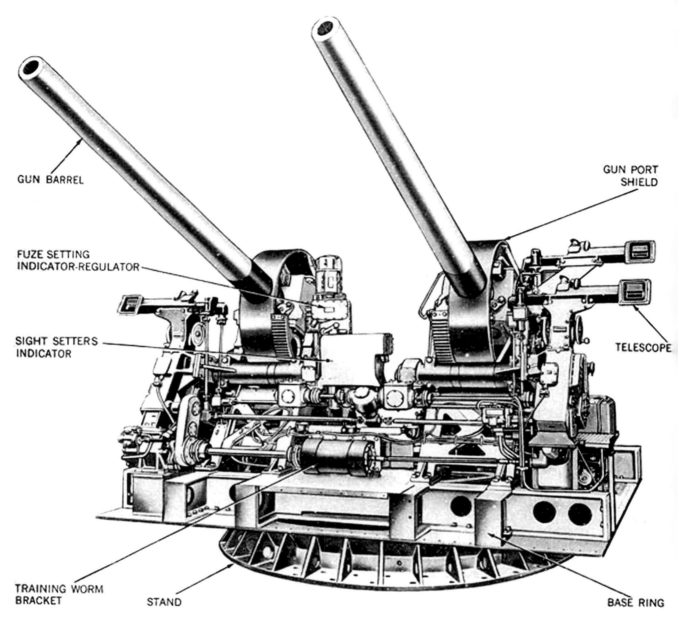

GUN BARREL

GUN PORT SHIELD

FUZE SETTING INDICATOR-REGULATOR

SIGHT SETTERS INDICATOR

TELESCOPE

TRAINING WORM BRACKET

STAND

BASE RING

In this image, we see all the interior features of the Mk 52 enclosed mount that housed two 5in/38 guns. The two guns operated and loaded separately; there was a hydro-pneumatic counter-recoil system to control the guns' recoil. The pneumatic (air) portion of the system pushed the gun back into battery, and the hydro (liquid) portion kept the air from leaking out of the system. (NHC)

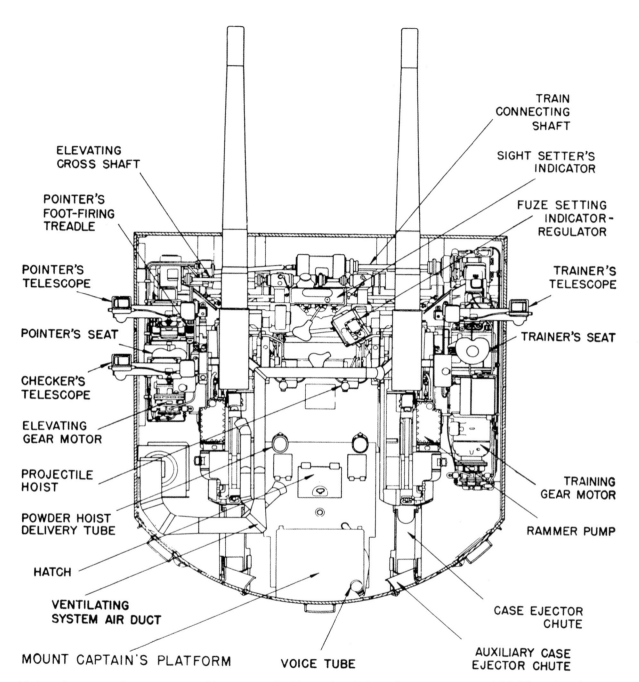

ELEVATING
CROSS SHAFT

POINTER'S
FOOT-FIRING
TREADLE

POINTER'S
TELESCOPE

POINTER'S SEAT

CHECKER'S
TELESCOPE

ELEVATING
GEAR MOTOR

PROJECTILE
HOIST

POWDER HOIST
DELIVERY TUBE

HATCH

VENTILATING
SYSTEM AIR DUCT

MOUNT CAPTAIN'S PLATFORM

VOICE TUBE

TRAIN
CONNECTING
SHAFT

SIGHT SETTER'S
INDICATOR

FUZE SETTING
INDICATOR-
REGULATOR

TRAINER'S
TELESCOPE

TRAINER'S SEAT

TRAINING
GEAR MOTOR

RAMMER PUMP

CASE EJECTOR
CHUTE

AUXILIARY CASE
EJECTOR CHUTE

Various features and some crew positions appear in this overhead view of a power-operated, Mk 52 enclosed mount that housed two 5in/38 guns. The big advantage with high-speed electric-hydraulic power drives for open or enclosed mounts is that they save space, weight, require less maintenance and are typically more reliable. (*US Navy*)

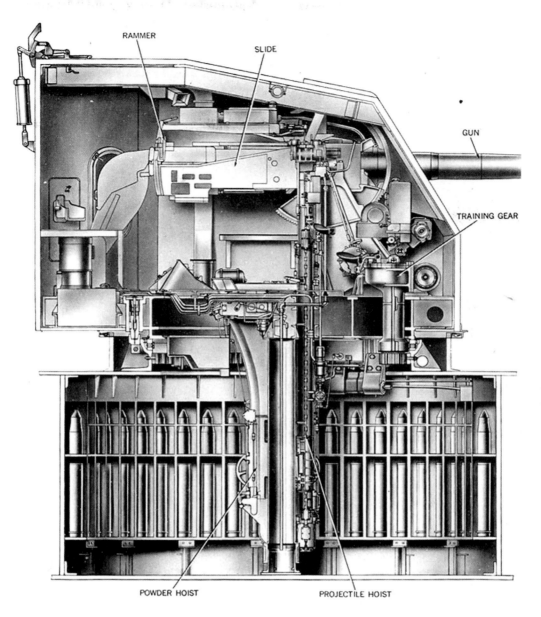

RAMMER
SLIDE
GUN
TRAINING GEAR
POWDER HOIST
PROJECTILE HOIST

(**Opposite, above**) The damage caused by a Japanese kamikaze to one of the 5in/38 Mk 52 twin gun mounts on the USS *Laffey* (DD-724), a *Sumner*-class destroyer. The 5in main battery enclosed power-operated gun mounts operated by remote-control from the gun director or locally from the mount's handwheel stations. (*NHC*)

(**Opposite, below**) A kamikaze struck one of the 5in/38 Mk 52 twin gun mounts on the USS *Douglas H. Fox* (DD-779), an *Allen M. Sumner*-class destroyer, on 5 May 1945. It stripped away the unarmoured gun enclosure, as seen in this image. Clips bolted to the base ring of enclosed gun mounts fitted under a stand firmly secured to a ship's deck to prevent an enclosed gun mount from tipping over in rough weather or when struck by a large object. (*NHC*)

(**Above**) From a US Navy manual can be seen the ammunition handling room and hoist mechanism that provided the rounds for a power-operated 5in/38 Mk 38 twin gun mount. Sailors removed projectiles and cartridge cases from wall storage racks and placed them into the powered hoist mechanism that brought them up into the gun house. (*NHC*)

(**Opposite, above**) With the New York City skyline in the background, the *Allen M. Sumner*-class destroyer USS *Harlan R. Dickson* (DD-708) heads to sea. Commissioned in February 1945, she arrived too late in the Pacific Theatre of Operation to see combat. The *Sumner* class had not the traditional single rudder but two rudders for improved manoeuvrability, a design feature that appeared on subsequent destroyer classes. (*NHC*)

(**Opposite, below**) Twelve units of the fifty-eight examples built of the *Allen M. Sumner* class were reconfigured as 'fast mine-layers' and received the prefix designation of 'DMs'. As mine-layers, they had an extended rack for depth-charges that ran along the main deck on either side of the ship's centreline. In this configuration, they received new hull numbers and were a sub-class labelled the *Robert H. Smith* class. (*NHC*)

(**Above**) On 12 April 1945, the *Robert H. Smith* class fast mine-layer USS *Lindsey* (DM-32) would be struck by two kamikazes that blew off 60ft of the ship's bow as well as the most forward twin 5in/38 Mk 52 gun mount. Despite the extensive damage visible in this picture, the ship was repaired and eventually returned to duty. The ship had started her time in service as DD-771 in August 1944. (*NHC*)

(**Above**) The successor to the *Allen M. Sumner* class of destroyers would be the ninety-eight units of the *Gearing* class, with an example, the USS *Higbee* (DD-806), pictured here. An improved version of the *Sumner* class, it was identical except that the hull was lengthened by 14ft. That extra length contained additional fuel tanks that in turn increased its operational range. (*NHC*)

(**Opposite, above**) With this model of a *Gearing*-class destroyer, we can see that the late-war threat posed by Japanese kamikazes had resulted in the removal of one of the ship's two quintuple 21in torpedo-tube mounts. In its place there appeared a quad 40mm anti-aircraft mount Mk 2. The same thing occurred with some of the late-war *Fletcher*-class destroyers. (*NHC*)

(**Opposite, below**) The open bridge of *Gearing*-class destroyers came from the square bridge arrangement eventually adopted for the *Fletcher*-class destroyers. The Mk 37 gun director with its Mk 25 radar antenna and the barbette it sits on is located directly behind the ship's enclosed pilothouse referred to in the Royal Navy as the 'wheelhouse'. The captain's quarters were located directly below the open bridge and pilothouse. (*NHC*)

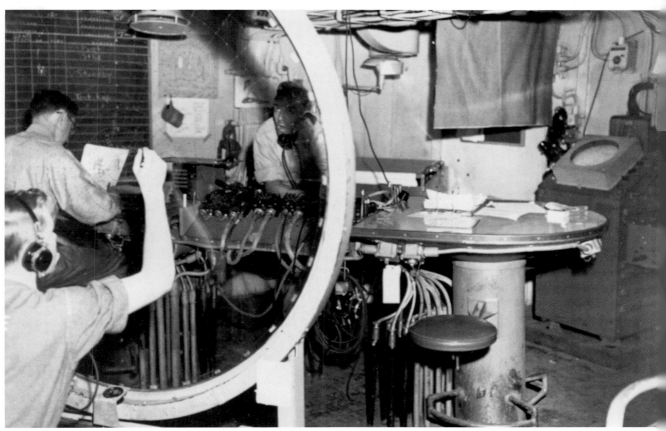

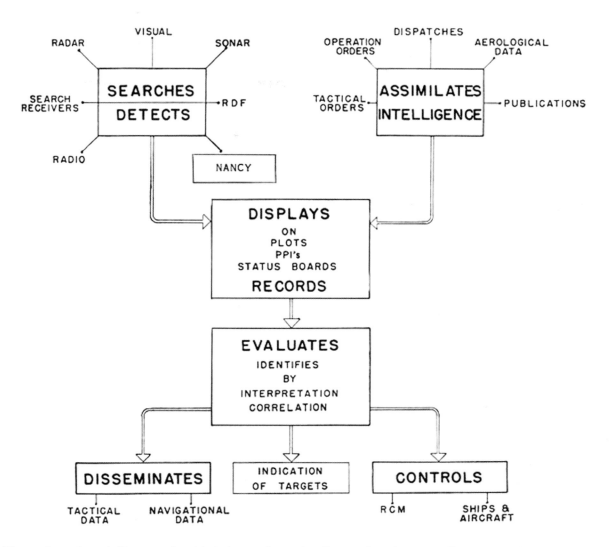

(**Opposite, above**) The two four-bladed propellers of a *Gearing*-class destroyer. They were 12ft in diameter, compared to the 11ft 6in propellers on the *Fletcher*-class destroyers. The original propellers on the *Allen M. Sumner*-class destroyers were three-bladed, but these led to serious vibration problems and cracking of the areas around the propellers and propeller struts also visible in the picture. (*NHC*)

(**Opposite, below**) In this wartime image, we the Combat Information Centre (CIC) on board a US Navy warship. They first appeared on the *Sumner*-class destroyers and would eventually be created on board earlier classes of destroyers during the Second World War. On the *Sumner* class and following destroyer classes, it was located in a large compartment in the ship's hull for added protection. (*NHC*)

(**Above**) From a wartime US Navy manual comes this line illustration of all the various inputs that flow into a Combat Information Centre (CIC) during an engagement. If the captain of the ship is not present in the CIC, then it is overseen '… by an officer who by his training and experience is responsible for the functioning of the CIC. He is the division officer of the CIC organization and as such is responsible for the training and welding of the CIC team into an efficient whole.' (*US Navy*)

Radar would prove to be the critical source of information for US Navy warships' Combat Information Centres (CICs) during the Second World War. The Japanese Navy had radar but never had anything comparable to a US Navy CIC. The US Navy wartime manual on CICs stressed that radar could be jammed or put out of action and hence human lookouts as pictured here remained extremely important for their input during battle. (NHC)

Chapter Four

Cold War Destroyers

In the immediate post-war era, the US Navy found itself confronted with a new threat: the Soviet Navy. The latter had jet aircraft, anti-ship missiles and a significant number of submarines. Making the US Navy's problems even more difficult at the time was a sharp decrease in funding, as had occurred following the First World War.

The US Navy informed the US Congress in 1948 that it required 192 destroyers on active duty to maintain a sufficient deterrent force. What Congress provided was just enough funding to keep eighty-two destroyers fully operational with another fifty-two in back-up status, as the US Navy lacked an adequate number of trained personnel to man the warships.

Except for five *Fletcher*-class destroyers retained as training ships and another eighteen converted into 'Destroyer Escorts' (DDEs), all the destroyers that survived the war went into the inactive reserve. The majority of the 134 destroyers that made up the immediate post-war inventory (both active and in back-up status) consisted of the *Sumner*- and *Gearing*-class destroyers.

Destroyer Escorts

A total of fifteen *Gearing*-class destroyers became DDEs. In that role, they retained only two of their original three twin 5in/38 enclosed gun mounts in favour of new ASW weapons. They also had four 3in/50 anti-aircraft guns divided between two twin open gun mounts. The individual guns themselves bore the designation Mk 26.

Despite the label of DDEs, those ships converted remained separate and distinct from the smaller and slower 'Destroyer Escorts' (DEs). Some DEs placed into service during the Second World War continued in service with the US Navy for a short time in the immediate post-war era.

Radar Pickets

At the beginning of 1945, the US Navy ordered twelve *Gearing*-class destroyers modified into radar pickets. In this role, they received the title 'Destroyer-Radar' (DDR). To support a host of new radars and other electronic devices, a new more substantial and stronger tripod went onto the selected destroyers. Eventually, twenty-four more examples of the *Gearing* class would become DDRs, the last twelve being authorized in 1952.

The electronic equipment that went into the DDRs took about nine months to install and cost more than a Second World War US Navy destroyer. As of 1960, the majority of DDRs reverted to the standard DD configuration. Six remained as DDRs until their eventual replacement by more modern destroyers.

Armament Changes

To improve the anti-aircraft defences of the *Gearing*-class-based DDR, the ships had six of the new 3in/50 anti-aircraft guns divided into three open twin gun mounts. The gun mounts themselves bore the designation Mk 27. The maximum rate of fire for the weapon mount came out to approximately fifty rounds per minute.

Control of the Mk 27 anti-aircraft gun mounts went to the Mk 56 fire-control director with the attached Mk 35 radar. The fire-control director could also control and direct the older-generation dual-purpose 5in/38 twin gun mounts in place of the Second World War Mk 37 gun director.

A US Navy post-war manual describes the background of the 3in/50 semi-automatic gun and its twin mount configuration:

> They were planned during World War II when a need developed for a rapid-fire gun with a larger explosive-projectile that could stop suicide planes or dive bombers. The 3"/50 mount was not completed in time to see combat in World War II, but it has proved itself very effective, and since World War II has virtually displaced its predecessors – 40mm twin and quadruple mounts – on combat vessels. It is generally used with relative-rate fire-control systems.

There was a significant problem with the post-war fitting of the 3in/50 guns in their twin mount configuration on US Navy warships as they had already been rendered obsolete by the latest advances in Soviet jet aircraft technology when introduced into service. They also lacked the firing rate, range and speed to engage enemy jet aircraft armed with nuclear weapons beyond the blast radius of their weapon/s. Only anti-aircraft missiles offered that ability.

Hunter-Killer Destroyers

In 1947 the US Navy began a programme aimed at improving destroyer ASW capabilities beginning with eight modified *Gearing*-class destroyers. Referred to as 'Hunter-Killer Destroyers' (DDKs), among their ASW weaponry was the power-operated and trainable Mk 14 Hedgehog and the new anti-submarine 'Mk 108 Rocket Launcher' fitted into a power-operated and trainable mount.

The Mk 108 rocket-launcher, also referred to as 'Weapon ALPHA', had been developed between 1946 and 1950 and first placed into service in 1961. The US Navy had envisioned it would replace the various types of Hedgehog weapons on destroyers, but this did not occur. It lasted in use with the US Navy until 1969.

These same eight *Gearing*-class destroyers had their wartime 40mm anti-aircraft guns and twin 5in/38 enclosed gun mounts replaced initially by two 3in/50 twin exposed gun mounts. Eventually, the 3in/50 exposed gun mounts would be replaced on the DDKs by two 3in/70 twin enclosed gun mounts designated as Mk 37.

In the Mk 37 gun mount configuration, the firing rate of the 3in/70 guns rose to ninety rounds per minute. One naval officer commented: 'When it did shoot, it shot a lot of bullets in a hurry.' However, bore erosion proved to be a severe problem until a cooler burning propellant was used in the cartridge cases.

In a post-war US Navy manual is a description of the ammunition fired by the 3in/50 Mk 26 gun:

> A complete round is 37.74 inches long and weighs 24 pounds (the projectile, with fuse, weighs 13 pounds). Since neither the mount installation nor the associated fire-control system includes provisions for fuse setting, only VT-fused projectiles are used in AA fire. Base-fused and point-detonated fused projectiles for surface fire are also available.

In 1950, the label DDK disappeared, and all such destroyers became DDEs. The latter label would be done away with in 1962, and all destroyers so titled went back to being referred to as merely DDs with their original weapon configuration restored, as the 3in/50 gun mounts (Mk 27 and Mk 37) as well as the Mk 26 gun itself did not live up to expectations.

Major Upgrade Programme

The threat from the Soviet Navy's submarine force grew in the 1950s. Lacking funding necessary to acquire new destroyers optimized for the ASW role, the Navy elected in 1959 to upgrade some of its wartime-designed destroyers. Under the programme, referred to as the 'Fleet Rehabilitation and Modernization' (FRAM) programme, it converted some of its wartime-modified general-purpose destroyers into specialized ASW platforms.

The programme came in three phases, labelled Mk I, Mk II and Mk III. The US Navy eventually cancelled the last phase. In total, 131 US Navy destroyers cycled through the Mk I and Mk II phases. Included were three *Fletcher*-class destroyers, thirty-three *Sumner*-class destroyers and ninety-five *Gearing*-class destroyers.

The First FRAM

The Mk I phase of the FRAM programme included only *Gearing*-class destroyers, extending their useful service lives by eight years. Initially only forty-nine *Gearing*-class destroyers were to cycle through the programme. In the end, the Navy put seventy-eight of them through phase I of FRAM. These included *Gearing*-class DDs, and previously-modified *Gearing*-class DDRs and DDEs.

FRAM phase I included a complete rebuild of the destroyer's hull and machinery. Everything above the main deck came off (except some of the twin 5in/38 enclosed gun mounts), replaced by new topside superstructures in one of three different configurations labelled Group A, B and C. This led to external configuration differences between almost all the phase I FRAM destroyers. Even within the Groups A, B and C of destroyers of phase I of FRAM there were external configuration differences centred around their twin 5in/38 enclosed gun mounts.

Without exception, all the phase I FRAM destroyers had the latest sonar and radar systems. The former was the keel-mounted AN/SQS-23 sonar, introduced into service in 1958. It replaced the Second World War keel-mounted SQS-4 sonar that had a maximum range of 15,000 yards (about 8 miles). The AN/SQS-23 had a maximum range of up to 40,000 yards (about 22 miles).

Weapon Array

Retained for the *Gearing*-class destroyers sent through the Mk I phase of the FRAM programme were two wartime twin 5in/38 enclosed gun mounts. Of dubious value against modern jet aircraft, they proved useful for shore bombardment and saw a great deal of use during the Vietnam War. As part of phase I of FRAM all the 3in/50 gun mounts were removed.

Due to the threat from North Vietnamese jet aircraft and patrol boats equipped with cruise missiles, some of the *Gearing*-class destroyers that had passed through the FRAM Mk I phase had improved anti-aircraft defence systems using the 'Ship Anti-Missile Integrated Defense' (SAMID) system. It consisted of the Mk 28 chaff-launching system, the 'Sea Chaparral' missile system, and a 'Shrike on Board' (SOB) anti-radiation missile system intended to home in on and destroy enemy radar systems.

The *Gearing*-class destroyers' two original centreline-mounted quintuple torpedo-launching mounts were replaced by two Mk 32 triple torpedo-tube firing mounts, one on each side. These were armed with homing torpedoes, primarily intended for the anti-submarine role. The original two fantail depth-charge racks were also removed.

ASW Rockets

In its search for a suitable stand-off anti-submarine weapon for its destroyers, the US Navy eventually settled on the Mk 112 Anti-Submarine Rocket (ASROC) launcher. Development began in the 1950s as part of the Mk I phase of FRAM II; the weapon entered into service in 1961. The launcher would be nicknamed the 'Pepper Box'.

The ASROC's power-operated launcher mechanism was trainable. Each of the ASROC's eight launching tubes contained a single rocket motor fitted with either a homing torpedo or a depth-charge warhead. The depth-charge could be equipped with a nuclear warhead if the need arose.

Once a warship's sonar detected a hostile submarine and its location, the ASROC Underwater Fire Control System (UFCS), designated the Mk 111 or Mk 114, took over. It tracked the target and automatically kept the launcher unit trained on the desired water entry-point. The ASROC had a minimum range of 900 yards, extending to a maximum range of 10,000 yards. Once the ASROC firing-control system had a solution, it fired a rocket motor.

At a certain point in its arcing flight path, the rocket motor separated from its respective warhead payload. The homing torpedo warhead's descent into the water would be stabilized and slowed by a drag parachute. The parachute provided decelerated the weapon, reducing the chance of any damage to a homing torpedo's sensitive electronic components as it struck the water. The depth-charges would be stabilized in their descent into the water by fins only.

ASW Drone Helicopter

To extend the range of its destroyers' weapons' range when engaged in ASW warfare, in 1962 the US Navy placed into service the Drone Anti-Submarine Helicopter (DASH) designated the DSN-3. Approximately 700 examples came off the assembly line. The unmanned nature of the relatively inexpensive drone helicopter allowed two to fit in a destroyer's aft onboard hangar. A DSN-3 launched from a helipad located next to the hangar.

The ASW drone helicopter had a range of approximately 35 miles, limited by the ship's tracking radars that helped guide it in flight. It was designed to carry two homing torpedoes with high-explosive warheads or a single depth-charge with a nuclear warhead, but the latter was never fielded. Without any attached weapons, the ASW helicopter's weight came to about 1,000lb and with weapons fitted approximately 2,300lb.

Maximum speed for the gas turbine engine-powered ASW drone helicopter topped out at 92mph with a typical cruising speed of 63mph. The drone had a ceiling of 17,400ft. In service, they proved difficult to control without a great deal of practice that tended to be unavailable, resulting in more than 400 lost in training flights. By 1971, the US Navy had given up on the programme and ended DSN-3 production and employment aboard destroyers in the ASW role.

FRAM II

The FRAM Mk II programme was more austere than FRAM Mk I. It included thirty-three *Sumner*-class and three *Fletcher*-class destroyers, extending their service lives by another five years. The selected ships' hull and internal components were generally brought up to the same level as the *Gearing*-class destroyers.

FRAM Mk II involved no wholesale removal of a destroyer's superstructures. Instead, regions were modified. The only significant superstructure change was the

Deep Water Sonar

A new sonar system installed on only the FRAM Mk II destroyers bore the label Variable Depth Sonar (VDS). It consisted of a hoist mechanism that lowered a streamlined transducer deep into the ocean. At a suitable depth, it could detect enemy submarines attempting to mask their presence from surface ship sonar systems by operating below layers of water of varying temperatures. These layers reflected or sharply-bent (refracted) sonar waves, making submarine detection extremely difficult by surface ships' standard keel- or bow-mounted sonar systems.

addition of a hangar and helipad at the aft end of the ship for two DASH helicopters as with the FRAM Mk I programme.

FRAM Armament

The FRAM Mk II destroyers retained all three of the wartime twin 5in/38 enclosed gun mounts along with the associated Mk 37 gun director. Like the FRAM Mk I destroyers, the FRAM Mk II destroyers had all wartime 20mm and 40mm anti-aircraft guns removed. They kept the Mk 10 or Mk 11 Hedgehog weapons installed after the Second World War but before FRAM Mk II took place. The FRAM Mk II destroyers never had ASROC fitted.

As with the FRAM Mk I destroyers, the FRAM Mk II destroyers had their wartime quintuple torpedo-launching mounts replaced by two trainable Mk 32 triple torpedo-tube firing mounts, one on either side of the vessel. They also had fitted two fixed Mk 25 single torpedo-launching mounts, one on either side of the ship.

The Mk 32 triple torpedo-tube firing mount had initially fired only an anti-submarine homing torpedo, the Mk 35. Later on, there appeared the longer-ranged Mk 37 homing torpedo suitable for use against both submarines and surface ships.

The Mk 25 single torpedo-firing mount initially fired only the anti-ship version of the Mk 16, a submarine torpedo adapted for destroyer use. Eventually it would be able to fire long-range anti-submarine homing torpedoes, the Mk 35 and Mk 37. The latter could be both an anti-submarine and anti-ship weapon.

After the Second World War and before FRAM, the *Sumner-* and *Gearing*-class destroyers had the Mk 2 launching system fitted that threw Mk 32 homing torpedoes over the ships' sides from a rack with air pressure. It was the same system employed by US Navy PT-Boats during the Second World War.

The End of the Line

Thirty-two *Fletcher*-class destroyers would eventually be passed on to friendly foreign navies, beginning in the late 1950s, where many would serve for decades afterwards. All the *Fletchers* disappeared from the US Navy inventory by 1971.

Like the *Fletcher* class, the *Sumner* class found itself withdrawn from US Navy service by the 1970s. Some went to scrappers; others became target ships to sink during training exercises, with another twenty-nine going to the navies of friendly foreign countries.

The last of the Second World War-designed destroyers, the *Gearing* class, were pulled from the US Navy inventory in the 1970s through to the early 1980s. By that time those still in service were serving as Naval Reserve Force (NRF) training vessels.

The last *Gearing*-class destroyer decommissioned in 1983 would be the USS *William C. Lawe* (DD-763). As with the two previous classes of destroyers, many of the *Gearing* class went off to friendly foreign navies for a second career.

Mitscher Class

In August 1948, the US Navy ordered four large experimental destroyers initially considered DDs and to be named the *Mitscher* class. However, during their construction, they were reclassified as destroyer leaders (DLs), a label harking back to the interwar-designed *Porter*- and *Somers*-class DLs.

The US Navy assigned the DL designation to the *Mitscher* class as it represented their envisioned employment as destroyer squadron flagships. Eventually, the US Navy would assign the classification DL to fifteen of its Cold War era-designed destroyers.

The four *Mitscher*-class DLs were commissioned between 1952 and 1954. With a length of 490ft and a beam of 47.5ft, they had a displacement of 3,642 tons. Crew complement ran to approximately 370 men.

As with all the wartime destroyers, the post-war *Mitscher* class exceeded 30 knots at maximum speed. However, their original powerplant proved so unreliable that some of those who served on the ships referred to them as 'an engineering dud'.

In 1955, the US Navy dropped the term DL for the *Mitscher* class, but for whatever reason retained the DL in their designation. To add to the confusion, the US Navy

---

Another Type of Frigate

To replace its aging inventory of wartime destroyer escorts (DEs), the US Navy came up with a modernized version, the first of which had its commissioning in 1963 with the last in 2004. Rather than keeping their original label of 'DE', the US Navy decided to refer to them as frigates (FFs). When equipped with a missile system they became FFGs.

Like the DEs of the Second World War, the post-war frigates were smaller and much more austere than the post-war-designed destroyer classes in order to keep their costs down. In total, 116 frigates came out of shipyards in many different classes, the last ship of which had its decommissioning in 2015.

---

decided to re-categorize the ships as 'frigates'. The new label change did not make much sense, as in most navies frigates were always smaller than destroyers. It took until 1975 before the US Navy adopted the practice of NATO navies in restricting the label 'frigate' to warships smaller than destroyers.

Mitscher *Armament*

The *Mitscher* class carried an impressive array of ASW weapons, but their main weaponry centred around their sensors and weapons in the anti-aircraft role. They were the first class of destroyers to feature a bow-mounted sonar instead of the keel-mounted sonars of previous destroyer classes.

In their original form, the *Mitscher* class had two new single-mount 5in/54 enclosed guns and two enclosed twin 3in/70 gun mounts as well as eight 20mm anti-aircraft guns. Eventually, the 3in/70 gun mounts came off along with the 20mm anti-aircraft guns to be replaced by other weapons.

The 5in/54 gun mounts came with the designation Mk 42 and had a firing rate of forty rounds per minute. Their ammunition feed relied on an automatic, dual-hoist gun-loading system that was hydraulically-operated and electrically-controlled.

The 5in/54 guns had a maximum range of 25,900 yards versus the 17,300 yards for the older-generation 5in/38 guns. On the negative side, they initially had an abysmal reliability record. One naval officer commented: 'The way to look at it would be forty rounds the first minute, and then zero or maybe twenty.'

In 1968, two of the four *Mitscher*-class ships appeared with a new surface-to-air missile (SAM) named the 'Tartar'. They became 'Guided Missile Destroyers' (DDGs) and remained in service until their decommissioning in 1978. The other two *Mitscher*-class destroyers had gone off to their decommissioning in 1969.

The RIM-24 Tartar Missile

The Tartar had entered US Navy service in 1960. It weighed 1,130lb, had a length of 15ft and packed a 130lb high-explosive warhead. The initial version had a flight ceiling of 50,000ft and a range of about 10 miles. Its introduction would not be trouble-free. One naval officer remarked: 'Its fire-control radar, the SPG-51, set new standards of unreliability!'

Once at sea, the Tarter suffered terribly from moisture, especially its electronics and circuits, a problem never truly anticipated by those who tested the missile on land firing ranges. In missile sea trials, it proved very vulnerable to electronic countermeasures (ECM) and showed itself to be easily overwhelmed when confronted by a large number of attacking aircraft. Despite having a speed in flight of Mach 1.8, it would already be too slow to engage ever-faster Soviet Navy jet aircraft when it entered service.

The first DDG would be a *Gearing*-class destroyer, the *Gyatt* (DD-712), fitted with a SAM system in 1956 as an experiment. The following year it would be re-designated as the DDG-1. No other Second World War-designed destroyer would become a DDG.

Forrest Sherman Class

Following the four *Mitscher*-class DLs were the eighteen *Forrest Sherman*-class DLs commissioned between 1953 and 1959. The class would be the first to have an aluminium superstructure to reduce weight. With a displacement of 2,800 tons, they had a crew complement of 233 men. The length came out at 407ft with a beam of 45ft. Serving into the 1980s, the last *Forrest Sherman*-class ship had its decommissioning in 1988.

The *Forrest Sherman* class went through various armament changes. They originally had three 5in/54 single enclosed gun mounts, four twin 3in/70 enclosed gun mounts, four individual 21in torpedo tubes, and one depth-charge rack. By the 1970s, the four twin 3in/70 enclosed gun mounts disappeared from all the ships in the class, and the four Mk 25 single torpedo tubes were replaced by two triple torpedo-tube firing mounts designated the Mk 32.

Eight of the *Forrest Sherman* class were eventually modernized to increase their capabilities as ASW platforms with the addition of ASROC and VTS. The addition of ASROC required removal of one of the ship's three 5in/54 single enclosed gun mounts. Four of the eighteen *Forrest Sherman*-class DLs had SAMs fitted and became DDGs.

In an extract from a US Navy publication titled *Black Shoes and Blue Water: Surface Warfare in the US Navy, 1945–1975* by Malcolm Muir, Jr is a passage by an officer who served on a *Forrest Sherman*-class destroyer:

> *Forrest Sherman* (DD-931) was a beautiful ship and a delight to command, but she was obsolescent when she was designed. Her 5-in/54s doubled the gun-power of any previous dual-purpose destroyer, but her fire-control equipment and radars were only marginally better ... Her habitability improvements, especially the air-conditioning, was greatly appreciated, but as a fighting unit, she ... represented the first step in the modern trend to build big, comfortable targets instead of lean, mean combatants.

Farragut Class

Commissioned by the US Navy between 1959 and 1961 were ten ships of the *Farragut* class. Some older reference sources also list them as the *Coontz* class. When first ordered by the US Navy they were labelled as all-gun frigates but eventually were re-classified as DDGs in 1975 as they all would have a SAM system.

With a displacement of 4,167 tons, they had a crew complement of 360 men. The length came to 512ft 6in with a beam of 52ft 4in. The last ship in the class had its decommissioning in 1992.

Instead of the Tartar SAM fitted to the *Mitscher* class, the *Farragut* class had the larger 'Terrier' SAM. The missile had a length of 27ft 1in and a weight of about 1,300lb. Flying at a speed of Mach 1.8, it had an effective ceiling of 40,000ft and a range of approximately 21,120 yards (12 miles). The original version of the missile had a 129lb high-explosive warhead.

The *Farragut* class also had a single 5in/54 enclosed gun mount, two twin 3in/70 enclosed gun mounts, two Mk 32 triple torpedo-launching mounts and ASROC. The lead ship in the *Farragut* class came off the slipway with an ASROC reload magazine in its superstructure. However, it made the ship top-heavy, and would not appear on any of the nine remaining vessels in the class.

Missile Systems

As time went on the two twin 3in/70 enclosed gun mounts came off the *Farragut* class to be replaced by two quad anti-ship missile-launcher units named 'Harpoon'. Initially entering US Navy service in 1977, Harpoon is an all-weather, over-the-horizon, anti-ship missile system with a low-level, sea-skimming cruise trajectory and active radar guidance. Also, the Terrier SAM on the *Farragut* class would be replaced by a SAM referred to as the 'Standard'.

Based on the earlier Tartar and Terrier, the Standard entered into service in the late 1960s. It offered advantages over the previous SAMs, including solid-state electronics and an upgraded inertial guidance system. These features improved the missile's effectiveness against low-altitude enemy aircraft and cruise missiles. Like its predecessors, the Standard would go through a progressive series of upgrades to enhance its reliability and operational parameters.

The Standard Missile

The capabilities of the latest version of the Standard appear in an extract from an online US Navy fact file:

Extended Range Active Missile (SM-6) provides an air defense force multiplier to the U.S. Navy to greatly expand the AWS [aviation warfare system] battlespace. SM-6 provides an extended range anti-air warfare capability both over sea and over land by combining a modified advanced medium-range air-to-air missile (AMRAAM) active seeker onto the proven Standard Missile airframe. This low-risk approach, relying on non-developmental items, supported an FY 2011 initial operating capability. With integrated fire control support, SM-6 provides the Navy with an increased battlespace against anti-air warfare (AAW) threats over-the-horizon.

Charles F. Adams Class

Between 1960 and 1964, the US Navy commissioned twenty-nine DDGs of the *Charles F. Adams* class. Based on the design of the *Forrest Sherman* class, they had a displacement of 3,277 tons and a crew complement of up to 333 men. The last ship in the *Charles F. Adams* class had its decommissioning in 1993.

With a length of 437ft, the ships of the *Charles F. Adams* class had a beam of 47ft. They were the last powered by steam turbine engines; all the follow-on US Navy destroyer classes would receive power from gas turbine engines.

The *Charles F. Adams* class had two single 5in/54 enclosed gun mounts as well as ASROC and anti-submarine torpedoes. For the anti-ship role, they came armed with the Harpoon. By the 1980s, the *Charles F. Adams* class was obsolete compared to the latest Soviet Navy equipment. A few ships in the class found themselves modernized under a programme referred to as the 'New Threat Upgrade' (NTU). However, in the end, the US Navy eventually decided to invest its available funding into a newer class of destroyer.

Spruance Class

As the US Navy's inventory of Second World War era-designed destroyer classes (updated by FRAM Mk I and Mk II) reached the end of their service lives, a new class of destroyers referred to as the *Spruance* took their place. In total, thirty-one examples of the *Spruance* class came out of shipyards between 1972 and 1983. The first had its commissioning in 1975. The last ship in its class would be decommissioned in 2005.

From a 1981 US government report on the *Spruance* class by the Logistic Management Institute is this passage on its many roles:

> The primary mission of the ship is to provide antisubmarine protection for attack carriers, antisubmarine carriers, amphibious forces, underway replenishment groups, and convoys. Additional missions include shore bombardment and gunfire support for forces engaged in amphibious assault or land warfare; countering surface craft within capabilities; anti-air self-defense; and collateral missions normally assigned to destroyers; surveillance, blockade, and search and rescue.

Spruance *Description*

The *Spruance* class had a displacement of 8,040 tons, making it the largest vessel ever labelled as a destroyer by any navy. They had a crew complement of 324 men. The length came in at 529ft and beam at 55ft. Due to their size, the *Spruance* class had both a hangar and helipad large enough to support two manned ASW helicopters that could engage both enemy submarines and surface ships.

The gas turbine engines of the *Spruance* class reduced both maintenance cost and the number of personnel required to operate them when compared to steam turbine engines. The gas turbines also provided quieter operation, making it much harder for enemy submarines to hear them. Their very high power-to-weight output allowed them to accelerate from 0 to 30 knots in one minute. Adding to the effectiveness of the gas turbine engines were controllable reversible propellers.

The *Spruance* class came with two of the 5in/54 single enclosed gun mounts: one forward and one aft at commissioning. Reflecting their ASW role, they had both an ASROC launcher and anti-submarine torpedoes fitted. Some of the *Spruance*-class destroyers were eventually fitted with two Mk 143 Armored Box Launchers, each armed with four Tomahawk Land Attack Missiles (TLAMs). The Mk 143 launchers were fitted on either side of the forward-mounted ASROC launcher.

The *Spruance*-class designers, anticipating the advent of new weapon systems, provided room for them on the ships before they were placed in production. These included the Harpoon, the 20mm Phalanx Close-In Weapon System (CIWS) and the Sea Sparrow SAM.

From an online US Navy fact file is a description of the Sea Sparrow SAM system:

> … it is a short-range, semi-active homing missile that makes flight corrections via radar uplinks. The missile provides reliable ship self-defense capability against a variety of air and surface threats, including high-speed, low-altitude anti-ship cruise missiles (ASCMs). It is widely deployed by US, NATO, and other inter-national partner navies.

Twenty-four of the thirty-one *Spruance*-class destroyers were eventually fitted with a sixty-one-cell Vertical Launching System (VLS) mounted in the forward section of the hull in front of the ship's bridge. Among the rockets/missiles that could be launched from the VLS included ASROC and the TLAM. The latter did away with the need for the two Mk 143 Armored Box Launchers as well as the Mk 16 ASROC launcher.

Kidd Class

In early 1979, the US Navy decided it wanted to buy four modified versions of the *Spruance*-class destroyers constructed for the Iranian Navy. Due to a recent change in that country's leadership, the American government had forbidden their delivery. The American Congress therefore went ahead and provided funding for the US Navy to buy them from the builder. Under new ownership, they became the *Kidd* class and entered into service in 1981.

Between 1988 and 1990, the *Kidd*-class destroyers were modernized with the New Threat Upgrade (NTU) to prolong their service life. However, anticipated costs associated with the continuing need to modernize them led to the US Navy deciding to pull them from service in 1999. The American government then approved their sale to a friendly foreign country, Taiwan. The four ships were delivered between 2005 and 2006.

Arleigh Burke Class

Cold War-era destroyers tended to be very specialized for their role, so in a significant change, the US Navy decided in 1980 that it wanted a new 'multi-mission' class of destroyers. The result would be the *Arleigh Burke* class listed as DDGs. The first example entered service in July 1991, just a few months before the December 1991 fall of the Soviet Union that ended the Cold War.

From an online article on a US Navy website there appears this passage on the *Arleigh Burke* class:

> Originally designed to defend against Soviet aircraft, cruise missiles, and nuclear attack submarines, this higher capability ship is used in high-threat areas to conduct anti-aircraft, anti-submarine, anti-surface, and strike operations. She is capable of engaging in air, surface and subsurface battles simultaneously utilizing a myriad of offensive and defensive weapons designed to support maritime warfare.

The US Navy plans called for more than eighty examples of the *Arleigh Burke*-class destroyers to be built. As of 2019, the US Navy has commissioned sixty-six of the *Arleigh Burke*-class DDG. Those already commissioned as well as upcoming examples come in sub-classes referred to as 'flights' that represent specific configurations of the ships' weapons and sensors, for example. Many earlier production flights have and will continue to be put through modernization upgrades, although they will lack some of the more advanced features of later-production ships in the class.

Arleigh Burke-*Class Description*

Reflecting the constant upgrading of the *Arleigh Burke* class, the displacement of the ship has grown from 8,184 tons from the first ships in its class to the latest examples that have a listed displacement of 9,600 tons.

The early-production examples had a length of 505ft with later flights having a length of 509ft. The beam on all the *Arleigh Burke*-class DDGs has remained at 66ft. Crew complements range from approximately 300 to as many as 325 personnel.

Unlike the *Spruance* class that had a superstructure made of aluminium to save weight, the *Arleigh Burke* class reverted to an all-steel superstructure for two main reasons. The aluminium superstructures on the *Spruance* class had suffered from severe corrosion and cracking. Another reason is that steel has a superior resistance to fire.

A steel superstructure on a warship also provides for more likely survival from blast pressure waves from ordnance detonating near a ship and the resulting metal fragments. Extra protection for the *Arleigh Burke* class also comes from 150 tons of composite and steel armour found in critical areas of the vessels such as the bridge and engine rooms.

The earlier-production examples of the *Arleigh Burke* class featured a helipad for helicopters to land and take off. Later models of the class were reconfigured to include a hangar large enough to store two manned ASW helicopters. The helicopters themselves have the designation 'Light Airborne Multi-Purpose System' (LAMPS).

Arleigh Burke-*Class Armament*

The impressive weapons array of the *Arleigh Burke* class originally included a single 5in/54 enclosed gun mount forward of the bridge. Later-production examples feature the longer-barrelled 5in/62 gun in the Mk 45 enclosed mount. Both versions of the 5in guns can be employed against enemy surface ships, close-in aerial threats, and provide shore bombardment support. The *Arleigh-Burke* class also has two Mk 32 triple torpedo-tube firing mounts.

For point defence of the ship from sea-skimming anti-ship missiles, the class has two 20mm Phalanx Close-In Weapon Systems (CIWSs) as well as the Sea Sparrow SAM. A small number of the *Arleigh Burke*-class DDGs have appeared with the 'SeaRAM' that incorporates the sensor system from the CIWS and replaces the 20mm multiple-barrel gun with an eleven-round missile-launcher unit armed with the Rolling Airframe Missile (RAM). According to an online US Navy fact file:

> The SeaRAM CIWS is a complete combat weapon system that automatically detects, evaluates, tracks, engages, and performs kill assessment against ASM [anti-ship missiles] and high-speed aircraft threats in an extended self-defense battle space envelope around the ship. SeaRAM can also be integrated into ship combat control systems to provide additional sensor and fire-control support to other installed ship weapon systems.

Supplementing the CIWS, the SeaRAM and the Sea Sparrow SAM on the *Arleigh Burke* class are two 25mm/87 Mk 38 Machine Gun Systems. The same weapon was mounted on the US Army's M2/M3 Bradley series as well as the Marine Corps' eight-wheeled LAV-25. Manually operated by a two-person crew on US Navy ships, the Mk 38 provides close-in defence against enemy patrol boats, swimmers, floating mines and various nearby land targets. A newer version can be operated from a console inside the ship but retains a manual back-up capability.

For the future, the US Navy is looking at a new weapon system for its *Arleigh Burke*-class DDGs referred to as the 'High Energy Laser and Integrated Optical-dazzle with Surveillance' (HELIOS). If the system does meet expectations, it will replace both the CIWS and the SeaRAM on *Arleigh Burke*-class DDGs.

Weapons and Control

Like the late-production examples of the *Spruance* class, the *Arleigh Burke* class has a VLS, in this case designated the Mk 41. The original model had ninety launching cells and the latest version ninety-six launching cells. These launching cells are capable of firing a wide range of weapons including a version of the Standard missile, employed to down enemy ballistic missiles. Other weapons that are launched from the Mk 41 VLS include the Tomahawk cruise missile, Vertical Launch Anti-Submarine Rocket (ASROC) and 'Evolved Sea Sparrow' missiles.

To control and manage all the various weapons on the *Arleigh Burke*-class DDGs, it would be the first destroyer class to feature the 'AEGIS Combat System', a description of which appears in the following passage from an online US Navy fact sheet:

> The AEGIS Weapon System (AWS) is a centralized, automated, command-and-control (C2) and weapons control system that was designed as a total weapon system, from detection to kill. The heart of the system is the AN/SPY, an advanced, automatic detect and track, multi-function phased-array radar. This high-powered radar is able to perform search, track and missile guidance functions simultaneously, with a track capacity of more than 100 targets.

While extremely impressive, the AWS comes with a very high price tag. From a passage in a May 1997 General Accounting Office (GAO) report is this breakdown on its costs:

> For example, combat and weapon systems account for about 55 percent of the cost of the latest version of the *Arleigh Burke*-class destroyer. Navy officials indicate that the Aegis combat system is a large cost – at about $235 million, or about 25 percent of the ship's cost. As a result, the Navy is examining ways to reduce the cost of combat and weapon systems while maintaining or improving the ship's overall capability.

Seen here in an early post-war view is the USS *Perkins* (DD-877), a *Gearing*-class destroyer commissioned in April 1945. She arrived too late in the Pacific Theatre of Operation to see combat during the Second World War. In 1949, she would be configured as a radar picket ship and therefore re-designated with the prefix letters 'DDR'. The radar picket duty would eventually go to specialized aircraft flying off aircraft carriers. *(NHC)*

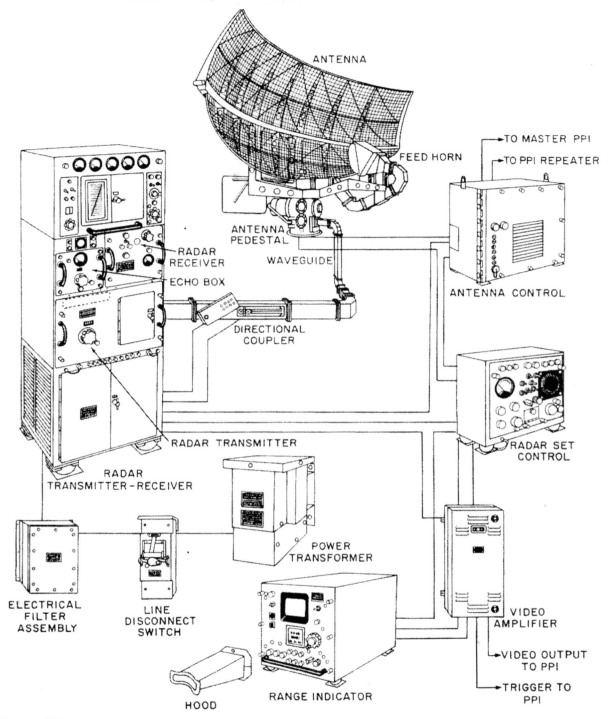

ANTENNA

FEED HORN

TO MASTER PPI

TO PPI REPEATER

ANTENNA
PEDESTAL

WAVEGUIDE

RADAR
RECEIVER

ECHO BOX

ANTENNA CONTROL

DIRECTIONAL
COUPLER

RADAR TRANSMITTER

RADAR SET
CONTROL

RADAR
TRANSMITTER-RECEIVER

POWER
TRANSFORMER

ELECTRICAL
FILTER
ASSEMBLY

LINE
DISCONNECT
SWITCH

VIDEO
AMPLIFIER

VIDEO OUTPUT
TO PPI

TRIGGER TO
PPI

HOOD

RANGE INDICATOR

From a US Navy manual is this illustration of a surface-search radar antenna and associated equipment that began appearing on early post-war destroyers. A passage from the manual describes the importance of surface-search radar: 'This equipment is not only invaluable for the location of the enemy task force, but is equally important in the location of surfaced submarines (it can detect even their periscopes), or for obtaining positions of ships in convoy.' (US Navy)

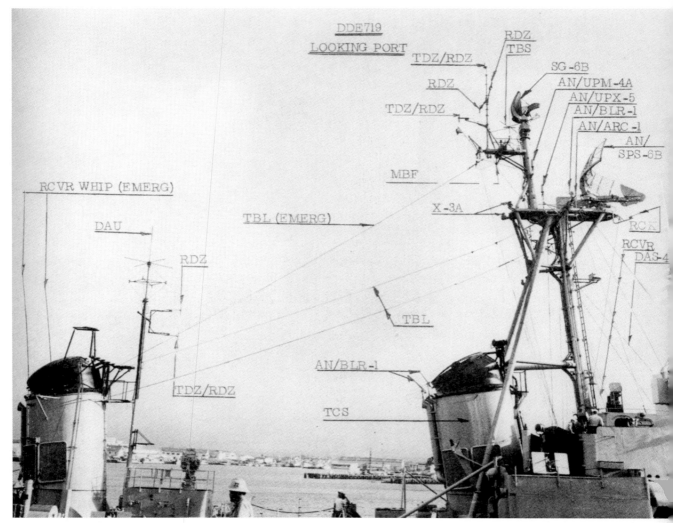

DDE719
LOOKING PORT

RDZ
TBS

TDZ/RDZ

SG-6B
AN/UPM-4A
AN/UPX-5
AN/BLR-1
AN/ARC-1
AN/SPS-6B

RDZ

TDZ/RDZ

RCVR WHIP (EMERG)

MBF

X-3A

RCK

DAU

RCVR
DAS-4

RDZ

TBL (EMERG)

TBL

AN/BLR-1

TDZ/RDZ

TCS

(**Above**) To support the increasing weight of the numerous radar antennas added to the Second World War-designed destroyers in the immediate post-war period, larger and stronger tripod masts replaced the original pole masts as pictured here. The vertical pole antenna positioned in front of the second stack with the prefix label 'DAU' is a High-Frequency Direction Finding (HF/DF) antenna nicknamed 'huff-duff', and intended to detect and locate Soviet submarines via their radio transmissions. (*NHC*)

(**Opposite, above**) In the foreground is a post-war added surface-search radar antenna on an *Allen M. Sumner*-class destroyer and above it an air-search radar antenna. Both are parabolic or barrel stave antennas. The pulses emitted by radar antennas travel at the speed of light (186,000 miles per second). By measuring the time it takes a radar pulse to bounce off an object and return to the antenna, range can be determined. (*Vladimir Yakubov*)

(**Opposite, below**) Shown here is the USS *Frank Knox* (DDR-742), a *Gearing*-class destroyer in the 1950s. Near the top of the ship's foremast is the large mattress-type SPS-29 air-search radar. It could detect aircraft at up to an altitude of 40,000ft. Behind the second stack is a post-war-developed SPS-8 height-finding radar. Due to its size and weight, it could not fit on the ship's masts. (*NHC*)

RADAR REFLECTOR

RADAR ANTENNA MOUNT

REAR ACCESS HATCH COVER

DIRECTOR OFFICER'S HATCH COVER

OPEN SIGHT

RANGEFINDER

SHIELD

TELESCOPE

TELESCOPE PORT CLOSURE COVER

FORWARD PEDESTAL

CARRIAGE

BASE RING

From a US Navy manual is this information regarding the Mk 68 director pictured: 'Basically, GFCS [Gun Fire Control System] Mk 68 performs the function as GFCS Mk 37 except that it has supersonic target speed capabilities ... The director normally tracks a target under automatic radar control ... The director is provided with heating, anti-icing, and defrosting equipment so that it can be operated effectively under widely varying climatic conditions.' (*US Navy*)

(**Opposite, above**) A close-up view of an SPS-8 height-finding radar on a *Gearing*-class destroyer configured as a DDR. According to a US Navy manual: 'Height-finding radars are three-coordinate radars. They are capable of discriminating between targets that are close together, and they are capable of measuring range, bearing, and altitude.' Due to their very narrow radar beams, they were not suitable as general air-search radars. (*NHC*)

(**Opposite, below**) The Mk 25 dish radar antenna that had replaced the Mk 12/22 radar antenna on the roof of the Mk 37 director would be in turn replaced by the SPG-53 radar antenna pictured here. Well aware of the high speeds possible with jet-powered aircraft and missiles, the US Navy began looking in 1945 for a replacement for the Mk 37 director. The initial effort resulted in the Mk 67 director that was not a success and was rejected in favour of the Mk 68 director. (*US Navy*)

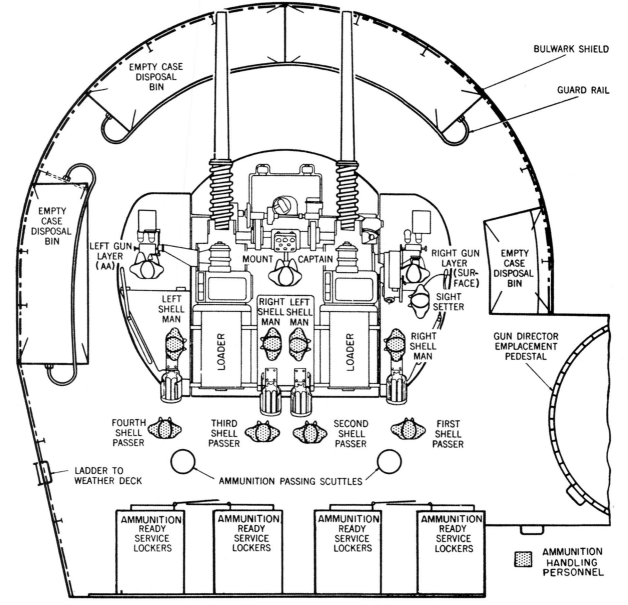

Labels in figure:
EMPTY CASE DISPOSAL BIN
BULWARK SHIELD
GUARD RAIL
EMPTY CASE DISPOSAL BIN
LEFT GUN LAYER (AA)
MOUNT CAPTAIN
RIGHT GUN LAYER (SURFACE)
EMPTY CASE DISPOSAL BIN
SIGHT SETTER
LEFT SHELL MAN
LOADER
RIGHT SHELL MAN
LEFT SHELL MAN
LOADER
GUN DIRECTOR EMPLACEMENT PEDESTAL
RIGHT SHELL MAN
FOURTH SHELL PASSER
THIRD SHELL PASSER
SECOND SHELL PASSER
FIRST SHELL PASSER
LADDER TO WEATHER DECK
AMMUNITION PASSING SCUTTLES
AMMUNITION READY SERVICE LOCKERS
AMMUNITION READY SERVICE LOCKERS
AMMUNITION READY SERVICE LOCKERS
AMMUNITION READY SERVICE LOCKERS
AMMUNITION HANDLING PERSONNEL

(**Above**) Visible here are components and crew positions on the twin 3in/50 guns in an open base ring stand mount Mk 27. The following description is from a passage in a US Navy manual: 'The 3-inch/50 rapid-fire RF guns are semi-automatic guns with automatic power-driven loaders.' The mount's maximum rate of fire would be forty-five rounds per minute. Primarily seen as anti-aircraft guns, they had a secondary role against surface targets. (*US Navy*)

(**Opposite, above**) The US Navy's planned wartime replacement for both twin and quad 40mm gun mounts was to have been the twin 3in/50 guns in an open base stand mount as pictured here. The gun mount itself received the designation Mk 27. Due to early post-war funding shortfalls, the weapon did not appear in service until 1948. The guns could reach targets at an altitude of 30,400ft. (*Vladimir Yakubov*)

(**Left**) Eventually the US Navy placed into service an enclosed version of the twin 3in/50 guns in a base ring stand mount labelled the Mount 33, as seen here. The guns' enclosure consisted of aluminium and had electrically-heated windows. By 1978, the twin 3in/50 gun mounts had been rendered obsolete as an anti-aircraft weapon and were pulled from service on destroyers.
(*US Navy*)

The US Navy considered the twin 3in/50 guns as only an interim solution to the threat posed by new post-war jet-powered aircraft and guided missiles. Instead, the service placed its faith in the development of twin 3in/70 guns in an enclosed mount, seen here on a *Gearing*-class destroyer. Unfortunately the weapon, which entered service in 1956, proved overly complex and unreliable, and would quickly be pulled from service. *(NHC)*

Developed in conjunction with the twin-mount 3in/50 guns and the twin-mount 3in/70 guns during the Second World War would be the radar-equipped Mk 56 gun director seen here. As with the gun mounts, post-war funding shortfalls delayed its entry into US Navy service. The first production examples did not appear until 1947. The Mk 56 could also act as the gun director for the 5in/38 gun mounts. (*Vladimir Yakubov*)

Experimented with by the US Navy on a few destroyers during the Second World War and eventually rejected would be the Royal Navy anti-submarine (ASW) ahead-throwing weapon known as the 'Hedgehog'. In 1950, the US Navy decided to mount an American-improved version seen here, designated as either the Mk 10 or Mk 11, on its *Sumner*- and *Gearing*-class destroyers. Both models were fixed forward-firing weapons. (*NHC*)

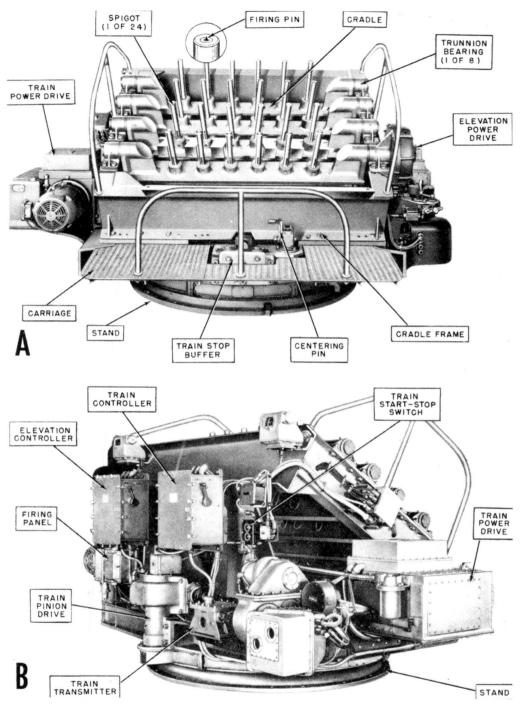

SPIGOT (1 OF 24)

FIRING PIN

CRADLE

TRUNNION BEARING (1 OF 8)

TRAIN POWER DRIVE

ELEVATION POWER DRIVE

CARRIAGE

STAND

TRAIN STOP BUFFER

CENTERING PIN

CRADLE FRAME

A

TRAIN CONTROLLER

TRAIN START–STOP SWITCH

ELEVATION CONTROLLER

FIRING PANEL

TRAIN POWER DRIVE

TRAIN PINION DRIVE

B

TRAIN TRANSMITTER

STAND

To improve the effectiveness of its existing anti-submarine ahead-throwing weapons the Mk 10 and Mk 11, the US Navy began fitting its Second World War-designed *Gearing*-class destroyers configured as DDRs or DDEs in the 1950s with the Mk 15 version of the Hedgehog pictured here. Its big advantage over the Mk 10 and Mk 11 Hedgehogs would be the fact that it was trainable. (*US Navy*)

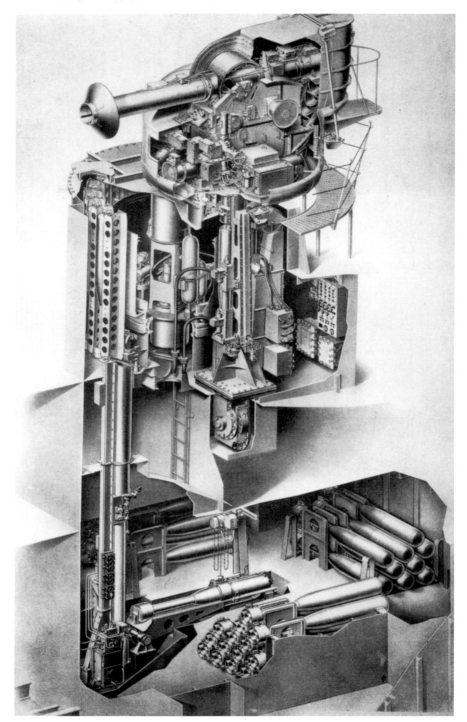

The next US Navy ASW weapon introduced into service for its post-war inventory of Second World War destroyer classes was the trainable base-ring stand Mk 108 Rocket-Launcher seen here, also labelled the 'Weapon Alpha'. The weapon fired a 525lb rocket-boosted depth-charge, capable of sinking a submarine with a single hit. The Mk 10, Mk 11 and Mk 15, by contrast, were more likely to just force an enemy submarine to the surface. (*NHC*)

(**Above**) In this photograph, we see the Mk 108 Rocket-Launcher in its enclosed mount installed on a *Fletcher*-class destroyer, employed post-war as an experimental test platform for new ASW weapons. Note on either side of the Mk 108 are Mk 10 or Mk 11 fixed Hedgehogs. On the muzzle end of the rocket-launcher is a circular blast deflector. In action, the Mk 108 could fire a round every five seconds to prevent the following round from being deflected by the preceding rocket's exhaust. (*NHC*)

(**Opposite, above**) The USS *Robert A. Owens* (DD-827) pictured here was a *Gearing*-class destroyer commissioned in November 1949. She had several prefix letter designations during her time in service. These included 'DDK' for a killer-type destroyer, and later became 'DDE' or destroyer escort. The ship is shown armed with a 3in/70 gun mount and the Mk 108 Rocket-Launcher. (*NHC*)

(**Opposite, below**) By the end of the 1950s, the Soviet Navy's submarine fleet was growing in both size and capabilities. Pictured here are two Soviet Navy diesel-powered submarines photographed by a US Navy patrol plane in 1957. Unable to acquire the funding necessary to build a new generation of destroyers optimized for the ASW role, the US Navy decided to rebuild and modernize some of the remaining Second World War destroyers of the *Sumner* and *Gearing* classes. (*NHC*)

Shown here is the *Gearing*-class destroyer
USS *Herbert J. Thomas* (DD-833), selected
for what became known as the Fleet
Rehabilitation and Modernization (FRAM)
#1. Those cycled through would be
stripped down to the main deck as seen in
this picture. The foremost twin 5in/38 gun
mount and the twin 5in/38 gun mount at
the stern remained. (*NHC*)

On display here is an example of a radio-
controlled Drone Anti-Submarine
Helicopter (DASH) stand-off weapon in
the hangar bay of a FRAM I upgraded
Gearing-class destroyer. Approved for
development in 1957 and tested in 1959,
the remote-control helicopter first became
operational in 1963. Despite high hopes for
DASH, the existing technology proved
unreliable and it never met any of its
expected operational parameters. (*NHC*)

In this image, we see a *Gearing*-class destroyer upon near completion of the FRAM I programme. The most prominent addition to the ship is the large hangar and flight deck forward of the aft gun enclosure. The hangar was intended to house two radio-controlled Drone Anti-Submarine Helicopter (DASH) stand-off weapons armed with conventional high-explosive homing torpedoes or a nuclear-armed torpedo. (*NHC*)

(**Above**) Placed into service at about the same time as the radio-controlled DASH stand-off weapon would be the anti-submarine rocket RUR-5 known as 'ASROC'. The trainable box-like launcher system for the rocket pictured here contained eight cells, each of which contained a single rocket armed with either a high-explosive homing torpedo or a nuclear-armed depth-charge. (*Vladimir Yakubov*)

(**Opposite**) Here is an image of the ASROC rocket with attached homing torpedo going through the loading process. From a US Navy manual: 'Because of its stand-off range [between 10,000 and 15,000 yards], ASROC makes it possible for the ASW ship to launch its weapons before the submarine is aware that it is under attack.' The conventional high-explosive torpedo warhead weighed just under 100lb. (*NHC*)

(**Right**) The firing process of the ASROC rocket/ missile appears in this illustration. The sonar information goes to the ship's fire-control system, which then automatically computes the anticipated target position, sets a time to separate into the timers on the airframe, and keeps the launcher aimed at the desired water entry-point. The rocket/missile can then fire when ordered by simply closing a firing circuit. (*US Navy*)

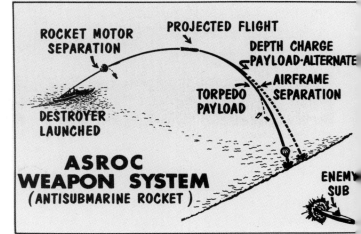

(**Opposite, above**) All of the 131 Second World War-designed destroyers that went through FRAM I or FRAM II had their centreline quintuple torpedo tubes removed. Their replacement was the three-barrel firing mount pictured here, the Mk 32. The torpedoes contained in the Mk 32 were small, lightweight ASW homing torpedoes intended to engage enemy submarines and not surface ships. (*Vladimir Yakubov*)

(**Above**) In this image of the USS *O'Brien* (DD-725), an *Allen M. Sumner*-class destroyer rebuilt and modernized under the FRAM II programme, we can see the trainable Mk 32 triple-tube torpedo-firing mounts on either side of the ship's centreline. Visible directly abaft the superstructure and the forward stack are the two single fixed Mk 25 torpedo-firing mounts, one on either side of the ship. (*NHC*)

(**Opposite, below**) A comparison photograph of FRAM I and FRAM II destroyers. The vessel at the bottom of the picture is a FRAM I conversion as only longer *Gearing*-class destroyers went through that phase of the programme. The shorter vessels are *Allen M. Sumner*-class destroyers cycled through FRAM II. A major external feature visible on the FRAM I destroyer and not the FRAM II destroyers is the ASROC launcher unit immediately aft of the forward stack. (*US Navy*)

Each *Gearing*-class destroyer that went through the FRAM I programme had one of three different main gun mount arrangements. The ships in Group A retained the two forward twin 5in/38 gun mounts as seen in this photograph, but not the stern mount. Those in Group B had only one twin 5in/38 gun mount forward and one aft. Those in Group C had only the forward twin 5in/38 mount. (*NHC*)

Located on the highest point of the rear deckhouse of all Second World War-designed destroyers cycled through the FRAM I and FRAM II programmes were the three black fibreglass domes seen here. These contained electronic support measure (ESM) antennas as part of the post-war WLR-1 ESM system of threat detection. They were the main sensor system for detecting incoming enemy anti-ship missiles. (*Vladimir Yakubov*)

All the *Allen M. Sumner-* and *Gearing*-class destroyers cycled through the FRAM II programme had the exterior portion of the Variable Depth Sonar (VDS) system fitted to their sterns. It consisted of a hoist that lowered the streamlined enclosure containing transducers, nicknamed the 'fish', into the ocean depth to be towed by the ship as it searched for its prey. The transducers in the fish could detect submarines hiding under the ocean's thermal layers that ship hull-mounted transducers could not. (*NHC*)

(**Above**) The long-awaited replacement for the twin 5in/38 gun mounts on US Navy destroyers would be the 5in/42 gun in the mount seen here designated the Mk 42. The weapon's development began during the Second World War. A scaled-up version of the 5in/38 gun, it had an automatic firing rate of approximately forty rounds per minute. (*Vladimir Yakubov*)

(**Opposite, above**) The 5in/54 gun in the Mk 42 enclosed gun mount is seen here on a destroyer; the dome on the mount's left was for surface fire. The mount could be controlled remotely or by a three-man crew inside the mount. The weapon's loading system consisted of a dual set of hoists that automatically and alternately load fixed rounds to the gun's breech from both sides. (*NHC*)

(**Opposite, below**) The first new class of destroyers ordered after the Second World War consisted of the four units of the *Mitscher* class, built between 1949 and 1954; an example is pictured here. These were commissioned with two of the 5in/54 guns in the Mk 42 enclosed mounts and four of the 3in/50 open twin mounts. For the ASW role, they also had two Mk 108 Rocket-Launchers known as Weapon Alpha. (*NHC*)

(**Above**) Following the *Mitscher* class came the eighteen units of the *Forrest Sherman* class built between 1953 and 1959. When ordered they were the last of the all-gun destroyers, each having three of the 5in/54 gun mounts with one forward and two on the stern. They also had four 3in/50 open twin-gun mounts, two Mk 10/Mk 11 fixed Hedgehogs, and four single torpedo mounts. (*NHC*)

(**Opposite, above**) Four of the eighteen *Forrest Sherman*-class destroyers were later reconfigured as guided missile destroyers (DDGs); the USS *Parsons* is pictured here. The two stern 5in/54 gun mounts were replaced with a single missile-launching firing unit that is barely discernible in this photograph. The surface-to-air missile (SAM) the ship carried was known as the 'Tartar'. (*NHC*)

(**Opposite, below**) The Tartar SAM, seen here on its Mk 13 launcher unit, measured approximately 15ft long and weighed 1,500lb. It was a smaller and shorter-range version of a larger SAM known as the 'Terrier' that had preceded it into service. Tartar initially had a range of between 2,000 and 15,000 yards. A later model possessed a range of up to 51,000 yards (29 miles) and could reach targets at a maximum altitude of 80,000ft. (*US Navy*)

Providing target-tracking and guidance functions for the Tartar SAM there were the SPG-51D circular dish radar antennas pictured here. The large rectangular black radar antenna is for an electronically-scanned array air-search three-dimensional radar system. The much smaller bar-like antenna on top of the air-search radar antenna is an IFF ('identification friend or foe') radar antenna. (*US Navy*)

After the *Forrest Sherman* class came ten examples of the *Farragut* class built between 1957 and 1961 with an example pictured here. Unlike the previous class of destroyers that had SAMs fitted at a later date in their career, the *Farragut* class was the first designed as guided-missile destroyers (DDGs). Instead of the Tartar, they would have the Terrier SAM. (*NHC*)

The Terrier SAMs pictured on their Mk 10 twin launcher unit individually weighed approximately 30,000lb and were 27ft long. Like the Tartar SAM, the Terrier went through numerous upgrades during its service with the US Navy. The final version had a range of 81,000 yards (46 miles) at Mach 3 to an altitude of 80,000ft. (*NHC*)

To provide the target-tracking and guidance functions for the Terrier SAM there was the AN-SPG-55 radar antenna as pictured here. It was the visible portion of the missile fire-control system designated the Mk 76. The heart of the system was a transistorized core memory computer designated 1218 and made by Sperry Univac. (NHC)

(**Opposite, above**) Next in line after the *Farragut*-class destroyers came the twenty-nine units of the *Charles F. Adams*-class (DDG) destroyers with an example pictured here. Built between 1958 and 1967, they were intended to be upgraded in the 1970s to reduce their vulnerability to the latest Soviet Navy anti-ship weaponry. However, the US Navy later changed plans and only three of the class received all the intended upgrades. The last ship in the class would be decommissioned in 1993. (NHC)

(**Opposite, below**) A new weapon introduced on the three upgraded *Charles F. Adams*-class (DDG) destroyers was the Harpoon anti-ship cruise missile seen here. Upon launching, the Harpoon flies a programmed, low-trajectory path to its intended target. In-flight attitude reference and mid-course guidance come from an onboard computer and stable element. It has a 500lb high-explosive warhead. (NHC)

139 063 + 24 005

(**Opposite, above**) An artist's representation of a sonar operator on a US Navy warship. The *Charles F. Adams*-class (DDG) destroyers had the AN/SQS-23 sonar. The system's transducers were located in a large dome at the bottom of the ship's bow to obtain the best sonar performance. With a range of 10,000 yards, its detection range exceeded that of the ASW weapons onboard the ship. (*NHC*)

(**Above**) The mainstay of the US Navy destroyer inventory during the 1970s and 1980s proved to be the *Spruance*-class destroyers with an example shown here. A total of thirty-one units came out of the shipyards between 1972 and 1983. They served from 1975 until 2005. They were the first US Navy destroyers powered by gas turbine engines. They had a displacement of 8,040 tons. (*NHC*)

(**Opposite, below**) The *Spruance*-class destroyers entered into service with the 5in/54 in the Mk 45 lightweight gun mount pictured rather than the older 5in/54 gun in the Mk 42 mount. Unlike the manned Mk 42 mount, the Mk 45 gun mount is unmanned. The gun crew resides below deck. A fully automatic gun, the rate of fire is between sixteen to twenty rounds per minute. It first entered service in 1971. (*US Navy*)

The large size of the *Spruance*-class destroyer provided it with enough room to house two manned ASW helicopters referred to as the Seahawk Light Airborne Multi-Purpose System (LAMPS) Mk III. It is a computer-integrated ship/helicopter system that allows for the helicopters to act as elevated platforms for both radar and electronic support measures. (*US Navy*)

An important addition to the *Spruance*-class destroyers' point-defence against anti-ship cruise missiles was the Phalanx Close-In Weapon System (CIWS) pictured here. It is the US Navy's first all-weather, automatically-controlled gun system. With its closed-loop spotting, it can track both its target and its projectiles in flight and automatically correct the projectile's aim onto the target. (*NHC*)

Another point-defence weapon on the *Spruance*-class destroyers was the Mk 29 NATO Sea Sparrow SAM seen here launching a missile. It provided the ships so fitted with a fully-automatic, lightweight, all-weather quick-reaction shipboard defence against aircraft, anti-ship cruise missiles and air-launched weapons. (*US Navy*)

There would be a more advanced sub-class of four *Spruance*-class-type destroyers taken into service by the US Navy in 1981. They were referred to as the *Kidd* class, with an example pictured here. The four vessels were originally ordered and completed for the Iranian Navy. However, with the 1979 Iranian Revolution, the order was cancelled and the ships were completed for the US Navy. They featured air defences not present on the *Spruance* class. (*NHC*)

(**Opposite, above**) The replacement for the *Spruance*-class destroyers, the mainstay of the US Navy's destroyer inventory, is the *Arleigh Burke*-class destroyer, with an example pictured here. Production began in 1988 and continues today. The major external design feature of the class not seen on any previous destroyer classes is the slanted superstructure, intended to reduce its radar cross-section. (*US Navy*)

(**Opposite, below**) Affixed to all four sides of the *Arleigh Burke*-class destroyers' slanted superstructure are large flat AN/SPY radar antennas, two of which are visible in this photograph. They are the visible portion of an automatic detection and tracking, multi-function phased-array radar system. The radar system can perform search, track and missile-guidance functions simultaneously, with a track capacity of more than 100 targets. (*US Navy*)

(**Opposite, above**) The *Arleigh Burke*-class destroyers' AN/SPY radar system is the critical element of their AEGIS Combat System, a centralized, automated, command-and-control (C2) and weapons-control system designed as a total weapon system from detection to kill. The main control room of the AWS in the Combat Information Centre (CIC) is seen here on an *Arleigh Burke*-class destroyer. (*US Navy*)

(**Opposite, below**) The most noticeable armament on the early-production *Arleigh Burke*-class destroyers is their forward 5in/54 in the Mk 45 lightweight gun mount. However, the majority of the ships' firepower is within two Mk 41 Vertical Launching Systems (VLS) that launch the ship's missiles. Pictured here is the forward sixty-one-cell unit with a smaller twenty-nine-cell example astern. (*US Navy*)

(**Left**) Sailors are carefully lowering a single missile storage and launching container into one of the two Mk 41 Vertical Launching Systems (VLS) on an *Arleigh Burke*-class destroyer with the help of an overhead crane. Twenty-one of the thirty-one examples of the *Spruance*-class destroyers had a single sixty-one-cell Mk 41 Vertical Launching System (VLS) on the ship's bow. (*US Navy*)

A Tomahawk cruise missile at the moment of launching from a Mk 41 Vertical Launching System (VLS) on an *Arleigh Burke*-class destroyer. Other missiles launched from the VLS include the Harpoon, the Standard (the replacement for the former Tartar and Terrier missiles), as well as the Evolved Sea Sparrow Missile (ESSM). (*US Navy*)

The replacement of the single forward 5in/54 on the later-production *Arleigh Burke*-class destroyers is the longer-barrelled 5in/62 in the re-designed, more angular Mk 45 gun mount. Developed as a lighter-weight, more easily maintained replacement for the previous gun mount, it has a twenty-round below-deck loader drum and is fired by a single crewman at a control console below deck. (*US Navy*)

Below decks on an *Arleigh Burke*-class destroyer is a Mk 46 lightweight torpedo being prepared for firing from one of the two main-deck-mounted triple-tube Mk 32 torpedo mounts. Besides the Mk 46 lightweight torpedoes, the destroyer class is also armed with the Mk 50 advance lightweight homing torpedo. (*US Navy*)

On 12 October 2000, USS *Cole* (DDG-67), an *Arleigh Burke*-class destroyer, was severely damaged by suicidal terrorists crewing a small explosive-laden boat. In response, the US Navy armed warships with machine guns, as pictured here, for defence in confined harbours and seaways. The weapon pictured here is an M2 Heavy-Barrel .50 calibre machine gun, the design of which dates back before the Second World War. (*US Navy*)

To provide more hitting power against explosive-laden small surface vessels, the US Navy began mounting a single-barrel, air-cooled, 25mm automatic cannon on its warships, including the *Arleigh Burke*-class destroyers. Early-production examples were manually-operated. The newest version, shown here, is designated the Mk 38 Mod. 3. It is stabilized and remote-controlled by a sailor at a console inside the ship. (*US Navy*)

One of the newest point-defence weapons on some of the latest *Arleigh Burke*-class destroyers is the SeaRAM seen here. From a US Navy online fact file is this description: 'SeaRAM combines the Phalanx CIWS Block 1B search-and-track radar and Electro-Optic sensor, along with its inherent threat evaluation and weapon designation capability, with a RAM 11-round launcher guide assembly on a single mount.' (*US Navy*)

Chapter Five

Post-Cold War Destroyers

O n 15 October 2016, the US Navy commissioned the first of what it had initially thought of as a class of thirty-two new cutting-edge technology DDG destroyers named the *Zumwalt* after the lead ship in its class. The lead ship received the hull designation DDG-1000. The *Zumwalt* class derived from earlier proposed destroyer designs. The first, labelled the '21st Century Destroyer' (DD-21) or 'Land Attack Destroyer', then evolved into what became the DD(X), with the 'X' in the designation meaning experimental.

The DDX eventually became the *Zumwalt* class, design work for which began in late 2005, with full-rate production starting in 2009. In a US Navy online fact file is an explanation of what the ship was supposed to be and the missions it was to fulfill:

> ... [it] will be capable of performing a range of deterrence, power projection, sea control, and command and control missions while allowing the Navy to evolve with new systems and missions. Stealthy, powerful, and lethal, the Navy created the *Zumwalt*-class to bridge from current needs to future capabilities, adding space and power accommodating systems not yet imagined but designed to counter adversaries that challenge us now and-in-the-decades to come.

The Reality

Unfortunately, despite high hopes that the US Navy had for the *Zumwalt* class, construction foundered due to failure to deliver certain critical technologies intended for the destroyers and ever-rising cost overruns. In 2009, a Department of Defense (DOD) official reported that the anticipated cost of each ship would be almost $6 billion, an 81 per cent rise in price compared to what the US Navy had originally estimated each ship would cost. The result was that only three of the *Zumwalt*-class destroyers were funded by Congress, and all have now entered US Navy service. The first entered in 2016 and the second and third in 2019.

Author Mike Fredenbury wrote in a 19 December 2016 article published in the *National Review* magazine and titled 'How the Navy's *Zumwalt*-Class Destroyer Ran Aground' presenting his thoughts on the ship class:

> The *Zumwalt* is an unmitigated disaster. Clearly, it is not a good fit as a frontline warship. With its guns neutered, its role as a primary anti-submarine-warfare

asset in question, its anti-air-warfare capabilities inferior to those of our current workhorse, the *Arleigh Burke*-class destroyers, and its stealth not nearly as advantageous as advertised, the *Zumwalt* seems to be a ship without a mission.

A Weapon Problem

One design feature that drove development of the *Zumwalt* class was its fully-automated, water-cooled, 155mm/62 6.1in Mk 51 gun referred to as the 'Advanced Gun System' (AGS), which would fire a round labelled the 'Long-Range Land Attack Projectile' (LRLAP) to a maximum range of approximately 96 miles. It was the United States Marine Corps and its Congressional supporters who pushed for this armament arrangement as they continued to believe that naval surface gunfire support still had an important part to play in future conflicts.

To help stabilize the AGS and to improve its accuracy when firing, the *Zumwalt* class was to take on water into its ballast tanks to lower the vessel into the sea. The class was planned to have the storage capability for 750 rounds of the LRLAP. The first significant snag occurred in late 2016 when the US Navy cancelled the LRLAP programme due to rising costs, questioning the *Zumwalt*'s intended primary mission.

With no current plans to replace the LRLAP, which had been specially designed for the AGS, the US Navy has a gun that cannot use any other NATO 155mm round. Plans continue on a search for a replacement round or possibly a new weapon to replace the AGS. Under consideration for replacing the AGS on the last ship in the *Zumwalt* class is an electrical-powered rail gun. From an online US Navy fact file is a description of how a rail gun works and its potential:

> The technology uses high power electromagnetic energy instead of explosive chemical propellants (energetics) to propel a projectile farther and faster than any previous gun. At full capability, the rail gun will be able to fire a projectile more than 200 nautical miles at a muzzle velocity of Mach-7 and impacting its target at Mach-5. In contrast, the current Navy gun, Mk 45 5-inch gun, has a range of nearly 13 miles. The high-velocity projectile will destroy its targets due to its kinetic energy rather than with conventional explosives.

New VLS

A dramatic design difference between the *Arleigh Burke*-class DDG and the *Zumwalt*-class DDG is the arrangement of their respective VLS. The two on the former consist of a large box-like enclosure that contains many individual canisters armed with a variety of missile types. The downside is that an enemy hit on either one of these enclosures might detonate the missiles within. Such an event could seriously damage a ship and at the least severely degrade a ship's offensive and defensive capabilities. To lessen the odds of something like that occurring, the *Zumwalt*-class ships have a different arrangement.

A description of the *Zumwalt* class's VLS arrangement appears in a June 2005 GAO report:

> The peripheral vertical launch system consists of the missile launcher, referred to as the advanced vertical launch system, and the enclosure for the launcher, referred to as the peripheral vertical launch system. The system is located on the sides of the ship to improve survivability, rather than the more traditional central positioning. The launcher is an evolutionary improvement on the existing design to ease the introduction of new missile types. The enclosure is a revolutionary design that prevents damage by directing explosions away from the ship.

Ship Description

The *Zumwalt* class has a displacement of almost 16,000 tons and a length of 610ft with a beam of approximately 80ft. This makes it forty times larger than *Arleigh Burke*-class destroyers. Reflecting the US Navy's emphasis on reducing manning costs by automation, the *Zumwalt* class requires a crew of only 140.

To reduce its radar cross-section, increasing its stealth capability, the ship has a 'wave-piercing tumblehome hull form', which the US Navy has never previously employed in a warship design. From a Raytheon website is a description of what the new hull form provided: 'The tumblehome (inward sloping) hull minimizes the *Zumwalt* Class Destroyer's radar cross section for enhanced stealth and survivability. Driven by a quiet and efficient all-electric propulsion system, the hull design optimizes speed, maneuverability, and stability while minimizing engine noise and infrared signatures.'

The sharply-slanted superstructures on the first two ships of the *Zumwalt* class are made from composite materials to reduce radar reflection. There were problems in sealing the composite superstructure, as well as its steep cost. These problems pushed the US Navy to have the third ship's superstructure made of steel. It is far less costly, but it does not offer the same degree of stealth provided by a composite structure.

The *Zumwalt* class is the first in the US Navy to employ an Integrated Power System (IPS) to generate all the ship's electric power. The electricity comes from electric generators powered by two Rolls-Royce gas turbine engines referred to as the MT30. It is the gas turbine engines that drive the *Zumwalt*'s two propeller shafts via electric motors, providing a maximum speed of 30 knots.

An artist's interpretation of what the US Navy expected the *Zumwalt*-class destroyers to look like when they entered the fleet. The original plans called for thirty-two units to be built to eventually replace early-production examples of the *Arleigh Burke*-class destroyers. With the *Zumwalt* class, the US Navy had the builder take the next step in reducing the vessel's radar signature by creating an actual stealth ship. (*US Navy*)

In the beginning, the US Navy saw the *Zumwalt*-class destroyers as primarily serving in the role of gunfire support. To this end, the ships were designed to have two 155mm long-barrelled gun mounts referred to as the 'Advanced Gun System'. Visible on this *Zumwalt*-class destroyer are the two enclosed mounts for the guns forward of the superstructure. (*US Navy*)

Besides the two Advanced Gun System mounts, *Zumwalt*-class destroyers have a new type of Vertical Launching System that has them arrayed around the ship's perimeter rather than grouping them in large structures to improve the system's survivability. In this artist's interpretation, one of the ship's point-defence missiles has intercepted an incoming enemy cruise missile. (*US Navy*)

With the US Navy's cancellation of the only round planned for the Advanced Gun System, labelled the Long-Range Land Attack Projectile (LRLAP), the *Zumwalt*-class destroyer's primary mission of gunfire support has gone. Instead, those built such as the example pictured here perform the same surface-war roles as the *Arleigh Burke*-class destroyers but at a much higher cost. (*US Navy*)

Such have been the ever-continuing cost overruns of the *Zumwalt*-class destroyers that the number ordered has been reduced over and over again. The original thirty-two planned dropped first to twenty-four, and then only seven. In the end, only three *Zumwalt*-class destroyers' construction was authorized. (*US Navy*)